Noam Chomsky

The Common Good

Interviewed by David Barsamian

Compiled and edited by Arthur Naiman

Odonian Press
Tucson, Arizona

distributed by South End Press
through Consortium

D0047601

Other titles in the Real Story series are listed on the inside back cover. You can find them at—or order them through—any good bookstore, or you can buy them directly from South End Press (800 533 8478 • www.southendpress.org • southend@southendpress.org) or from us, Odonian Press (800 REAL STORY • www.realstory.com • odonian@realstory.com). Quantity discounts are available.

Sales to the book trade are through Consortium (800 283 3572 • www.cbsd.com • consortium@cbsd.com). Real Story books are also available from wholesalers.

*Interviews conducted by **David Barsamian** on February 6 and 9, June 7 and December 13 and 17, 1996, and February 4 and 7, 1997.*

*Transcription: **Sandy Adler** (Boulder CO)*

*Compilation, editing, design, layout and index: **Arthur Naiman***

*Proofreading: **Susan McCallister** (Berkeley CA)*

*Cover photo: **Elaine Brière** (Mission, British Columbia)*

*Logistics: **Richard Korol** (Eugene OR)*

*Fonts: Questions, notes, etc: **Optima**. Answers: **Slimbach Medium**. Heads, etc: **Liberty** (fittingly)*

Printed in Canada   Fifth printing—August, 2003

Library of Congress Catalog Card Number: 98-36584

A Real Story book from Odonian Press

Odonian Press gets its name from Ursula Le Guin's wonderful novel *The Dispossessed*. The last story in her book *The Wind's Twelve Quarters* also features the Odonians (and Odo herself).

Odonian Press donates at least 10% of its aftertax income to organizations working for social justice.

TABLE OF CONTENTS

Editor's note	*4*
The common good	
That dangerous radical Aristotle	*5*
Equality	*8*
Libraries	*11*
Freedom	*13*
On the home front	
The myth of hard times	*24*
Corporate welfare	*29*
Crime: suites vs. streets	*34*
The media	*41*
More money, fewer voters	*53*
Is corporate power invincible?	*56*
Around the world	
Is globalization inevitable?	*65*
The myth of Third World debt	*74*
Mexico, Cuba and Guatemala	*77*
Brazil, Argentina and Chile	*80*
The Mideast	*87*
East Timor	*97*
India	*100*
International organizations	*114*
The US left (and imitations thereof)	
Are left and right meaningful terms?	*120*
The narcissism of small differences	*122*
Postmodernism	*125*
Excommunicated by the illuminati	*129*
What you can do	
Signs of progress (and not)	*134*
Resistance	*139*
The magic answer	*149*
Manufacturing dissent	*153*
Some organizations worth supporting	*159*
Sources for current information	*170*
Notes	*172*
Index	*176*
Alternative Radio tapes & transcripts	*191*
Other Real Story books	*192*

EDITOR'S NOTE

This book was compiled from seven long interviews David Barsamian did with Noam Chomsky. After I reorganized and edited the material, they made corrections and changes to the manuscript. Chomsky also added a lot of new material, and provided many sources for current information.

Barsamian's questions appear in this font, **Chomsky's** responses in this one. I've added some explanatory notes [inside square brackets]. If you run across a term or a name you don't recognize, check the index for the first page on which it appears.

If this book angers, depresses or appalls you—and if it doesn't, check your pulse—see *What you can do* (p. 134) and *Some organizations worth supporting* (p. 159).

Barsamian's interviews are broadcast as the Alternative Radio series on 125 stations worldwide. For information about tapes and/or transcripts of interviews and talks by Chomsky and many other interesting speakers, see p. 191.

Noam Chomsky was born in Philadelphia in 1928. Since 1955, he's taught linguistics—a field his theories have revolutionized—and philosophy at MIT. He's received countless honors and awards.

Chomsky has written many books on social issues, and his political talks have been heard, typically by standing-room-only audiences, all over the country and the globe. In a saner world, his tireless efforts to promote justice would have long ago won him the Nobel Peace Prize.

Arthur Naiman

THE COMMON GOOD

THAT DANGEROUS RADICAL ARISTOTLE

Early in January 1997, you gave a talk at a conference in Washington DC. It was sponsored by several organizations, including the Progressive Caucus, a group of about fifty liberal and radical members of Congress. What did you think of the conference?

I was pretty encouraged by what I saw of it. There was a good, lively atmosphere, a lot of vitality. A dominant feeling there—with which I agree—was that a considerable majority of Americans are more or less in favor of New Deal-style liberalism. That's remarkable, since most Americans never hear *anybody* advocating that position.

Supposedly, the market has proved that the L-word is bad—that's what's drummed into everybody's head all the time. Yet many people in the Progressive Caucus who publicly stood for New Deal positions—like Sen. Paul Wellstone [D–Minn.], Rep. Jim McGovern [D–Mass.] and others—won their elections. The Progressive Caucus actually grew after the 1996 election.

Now I don't think New Deal liberalism is the end of the road...by any means. But its achievements, which are the result of a lot of popular struggle, are worth defending and expanding.

Your talk was entitled *The Common Good.*

That title was given to me, and since I'm a nice, obedient type, that's what I talked about. I started from the beginning, with Aristotle's *Politics,* which is the foundation of most subsequent political theory.

Aristotle took it for granted that a democracy should be fully participatory (with some notable exceptions, like women and slaves) and that it should aim for the common good. In order to achieve that, it has to ensure relative equality, "moderate and sufficient property" and "lasting prosperity" for everyone.

In other words, Aristotle felt that if you have extremes of poor and rich, you can't talk seriously about democracy. Any true democracy has to be what we call today a welfare state—actually, an extreme form of one, far beyond anything envisioned in this century.

(When I pointed this out at a press conference in Majorca, the headlines in the Spanish papers read something like, *If Aristotle were alive today, he'd be denounced as a dangerous radical.* That's probably true.)

The idea that great wealth and democracy can't exist side by side runs right up through the Enlightenment and classical liberalism, including major figures like de Tocqueville, Adam Smith, Jefferson and others. It was more or less assumed.

Aristotle also made the point that if you have, in a perfect democracy, a small number of very rich people and a large number of very poor people, the poor will use their democratic rights to take property away from the rich. Aristotle regarded that as unjust, and proposed two possible solutions: reducing poverty (which is what he recommended) or reducing democracy.

James Madison, who was no fool, noted the same problem, but unlike Aristotle, he aimed to reduce democracy rather than poverty. He believed that the primary goal of government is "to protect the minority of the opulent against the majority." As his colleague John Jay was fond of putting it, "The people who own the country ought to govern it."

Madison feared that a growing part of the population, suffering from the serious inequities of the society, would "secretly sigh for a more equal distribution of [life's] blessings." If they had democratic power, there'd be a danger they'd do something more than sigh. He discussed this quite explicitly at the Constitutional Convention, expressing his concern that the poor majority would use its power to bring about what we would now call land reform.

So he designed a system that made sure democracy couldn't function. He placed power in the hands of the "more capable set of men," those who hold "the wealth of the nation." Other citizens were to be marginalized and factionalized in various ways, which have taken a variety of forms over the years: fractured political constituencies, barriers against unified working-class action and cooperation, exploitation of ethnic and racial conflicts, etc.

(To be fair, Madison was *pre*capitalist and his "more capable set of men" were supposed to be "enlightened statesmen" and "benevolent philosophers," not investors and corporate executives trying to maximize their own wealth regardless of the effect that has on other people. When Alexander Hamilton and his followers began to turn the US into a capitalist state, Madison was pretty appalled. In my opinion, he'd be an anticapitalist if he were alive today—as would Jefferson and Adam Smith.)

It's extremely unlikely that what are now called "inevitable results of the market" would ever be tolerated in a truly democratic society. You can take Aristotle's path and make sure that almost everyone has "moderate and sufficient property"— in other words, is what he called "middle-class." Or you can take Madison's path and limit the functioning of democracy.

Throughout our history, political power has been, by and large, in the hands of those who own the country. There have been some limited variations on that theme, like the New Deal. FDR had to respond to the fact that the public was not going to tolerate the existing situation. He left power in the hands of the rich, but bound them to a kind of social contract. That was nothing new, and it will happen again.

EQUALITY

Should we strive merely for equality of opportunity, or for equality of outcome, where everyone ends up in more or less the same economic condition?

Many thinkers, beginning with Aristotle, have held that equality of outcome should be a major goal of any just and free society. (They didn't mean identical outcomes, but at least relatively equal conditions.)

Acceptance of radical inequality of outcome is a sharp departure from the core of the humane liberal tradition as far back as it goes. In fact, Adam Smith's advocacy of markets was based on the assumption that under conditions of perfect liberty, free markets would lead to perfect equality of outcome, which he believed was a good thing.

Another grand figure of the pantheon, de Tocqueville, admired the relative equality he thought he saw in American society. (He exaggerated it considerably, but let's put aside the question of whether his perceptions were accurate.) He pointed out quite explicitly that if a "permanent inequality of conditions" ever developed, that would be the death of democracy.

Incidentally, in other parts of his work that aren't widely quoted, de Tocqueville condemned the "manufacturing aristocracy" that was growing up under his eyes in the US, which he called "one of the harshest" in history. He said that if it ever got power, we'd be in deep trouble. Jefferson and other Enlightenment figures had the same fear. Unfortunately, it happened far beyond their worst nightmares.

Ron Daniels, who's director of the Center for Constitutional Rights in New York, uses the metaphor of two runners in a race: One begins at the starting line and the other begins five feet from the finish line.

That's a good analogy, but I don't think it gets to the main point. It's true that there's nothing remotely like equality of opportunity in this country, but even if there were, the system would *still* be intolerable.

Suppose you have two runners who start at exactly the same point, have the same sneakers, and so on. One finishes first and gets everything he wants; the other finishes second and starves to death.

One of the mechanisms to address inequality is affirmative action. What do you think of it?

Many societies just take it for granted. In India, for example, a sort of affirmative action system called *reservations* was instituted back in the late 1940s, at the time of independence, in an effort to try to overcome very long-standing and deep-seated caste and gender differences.

Any such system is going to impose hardships on some people, in order (one hopes) to develop a more equitable and just society for the future. How it works as a practical matter can be tricky. I don't think there are any simple mechanical rules for it.

The attack on affirmative action is, to a large extent, an attempt to justify the oppressive, discriminatory patterns that existed in the past. On the other hand, affirmative action should certainly be designed so that it doesn't harm poor people who don't happen to be in the categories designated for support.

That can be done. There have been very effective applications of affirmative action—in the universities, the construction industry, the public service field and elsewhere. If you look in detail, you find plenty of things to criticize, but the main thrust of the program is humane and appropriate.

LIBRARIES

Libraries were very important to your intellectual development when you were a kid, weren't they?

I used to haunt the main public library in downtown Philadelphia, which was extremely good. That's where I read all the offbeat anarchist and left-Marxist literature I'm always quoting. Those were days when people read, and used the libraries very extensively. Public services were richer in many ways back in the late '30s and early '40s.

I think that's one of the reasons why poor, even unemployed people living in slums seemed more hopeful back then. Maybe this is sentimentality, and it involves comparing a child's perceptions and an adult's, but I think it's true.

Libraries were one of the factors. They weren't just for educated people—a lot of people used them. That's much less true now.

I'll tell you why I asked. Recently I went back to visit the public library I used when I was a kid, on 78th and York in New York. I hadn't been there in thirty-five years, and it's now in one of the richest districts in the country.

I discovered they had very few political books. When the librarian explained that branch libraries carry mostly bestsellers, I told him I'd be happy to donate some of our books.

He expressed mild interest and suggested I fill out a form. When I went over to the desk to get one, I found out that it costs 30¢ to recommend a book you think the library should purchase!

It sounds similar to what you find in the publications industry in general, including bookstores. I travel a lot and often get stuck in some airport or other...because it's snowing in Chicago, say. I used to be able to find something I wanted to read in the airport bookstore—maybe a classic, maybe something current. Now it's almost impossible. (It's not just in the US, by the way. I was stuck at the airport in Naples not long ago and the bookstore there was awful too.)

I think it's mostly just plain market pressures. Bestsellers move fast, and it costs money to keep books around that don't sell very quickly. Changes in the tax laws have exacerbated the problem, by making it more expensive for publishers to hold inventory, so books tend to get remaindered [sold off at cost and put out-of-print] much sooner.

I think political books are being harmed by this— if you go into the big chains, which pretty much dominate bookselling now, you certainly don't find many of them—but the same thing is true of most books. I don't think it's political censorship.

The right wing is promoting the idea of charging people to use the library.

That's part of the whole idea of redesigning society so that it just benefits the wealthy. Notice that they aren't calling for terminating the Pentagon. They're not crazy enough to believe it's defending us from the Martians or somebody, but they understand very clearly that it's a subsidy for the rich. So the Pentagon is fine, but libraries aren't.

Lexington, the Boston suburb where I live, is an upper-middle-class, professional town where people are willing and able to contribute to the library. I give money to it and use it, and benefit from the fact that it's quite good.

But I don't like the fact that zoning laws and inadequate public transportation virtually guarantee that only rich people can live in Lexington. In poorer neighborhoods, few people have enough money to contribute to the library, or time to use it, or knowledge of what to look for once they're there.

Let me tell you a dismal story. One of my daughters lived in a declining old mill town. It's not a horrible slum, but it's fading away. The town happens to have a rather nice public library—not a wonderful collection, but good things for children. It's nicely laid out, imaginatively designed, staffed by a couple of librarians.

I went with her kids on a Saturday afternoon, and nobody was there except a few children of local professional families. Where are the kids who ought to be there? I don't know, probably watching television, but going to the library just isn't the kind of thing they do.

It *was* the kind of thing you did if you were a working-class person fifty or sixty years ago. Emptying people's minds of the ability, or even the desire, to gain access to cultural resources— that's a tremendous victory for the system.

FREEDOM

The word *freedom* has become virtually synonymous with *capitalism,* as in the title of Milton Friedman's book, *Capitalism and Freedom.*

It's an old scam. Milton Friedman is smart enough to know that there's never been anything remotely resembling capitalism, and that if there were, it wouldn't survive for three seconds—mostly because business wouldn't let it. Corporations insist on powerful governments to protect them from market discipline, and their very existence is an attack on markets.

All this talk about capitalism and freedom has got to be a conscious fraud. As soon as you move into the real world, you see that nobody could actually believe that nonsense.

Dwayne Andreas, CEO of ADM [Archer Daniels Midland, a major NPR and PBS sponsor that calls itself "Supermarket to the World"] was quoted as saying, "There's not one grain of anything in the world that is sold in the free market. Not one! The only place you see a free market is in the speeches of politicians."

It must have been an internal memo or talk—that's not the kind of thing you tell the public. But in general it's true. As the United Nations Development Program put it, "survival in agricultural markets depends less on comparative advantage than on comparative access to subsidies."

Two technical economists in Holland found that *every single one* of the hundred largest transnational corporations on *Fortune* magazine's list has benefited from the industrial policy of its home country, and that at least twenty of them wouldn't have even survived if their governments hadn't taken them over or given them large subsidies when they were in trouble.

There was a front-page article in the *Boston Globe* that talked about our passing Japan in semiconductor production. It said that we've just seen "one of the great role reversals of the modern era—the transformation of Japan from behemoth to bungler....Japan's government-guided effort to dominate the chip industry, for example, was turned back. The US share of global chip production, which sank below Japan's in 1985, jumped back ahead of it in 1993 and has remained there." The article quoted Edward Lincoln, economic advisor to former US Ambassador to Japan Walter Mondale, as saying, "The lesson of the 1990s is that all nations obey the same economic laws."

What actually happened? During the 1980s, the Reagan-Bush administrations forced Japan to raise prices for chips and to guarantee US producers a share in Japanese markets. They also poured a lot of money into our own industry, through the military system and through Sematech, a government-industry consortium that was restricted to US companies. Because of this large-scale state intervention, the US did indeed regain control of the more sophisticated end of the microprocessor market.

Japan then announced it was starting up a new government-industry consortium for semiconductors in an effort to compete. (Some US corporations are to participate in Japan's projects in the new age that some business economists call "alliance capitalism.") Obviously, neither action had anything to do with the laws of the market.

The Mexican bailout is another example. The big investment firms in New York could have taken a beating if Mexico defaulted on its loans, or paid short-term loans in devalued pesos, as it was legally entitled to do. But they got the American public to guarantee their losses—as usual.

You can make as much money as you want, but if you get into trouble, it's the taxpayers' responsibility to fix things. Under capitalism, investment is supposed to be as risk-free as possible. No corporation wants free markets—what they want is power.

Another of the many areas where freedom and capitalism collide is what's laughably called *free trade*. About 40% of US trade is estimated to be internal to individual corporations. If a US auto manufacturer ships a part from Indiana to Illinois, that isn't called trade; if it ships the same part from Illinois to northern Mexico, it *is* called trade—it's considered an export when it leaves and an import when it comes back.

But that's nothing more than exploiting cheaper labor, avoiding environmental regulations and playing games about where you pay your taxes. This sort of activity also accounts for similar or even higher proportions of trade in other industrial countries. Furthermore, strategic alliances among firms play an increasing role in administration of the global economy.

So talk about "the growth in world trade" is largely a joke. What's growing is complicated interactions among transnational corporations— centrally managed institutions that really amount to private command economies.

The hypocrisy is pervasive. For example, free-trade boosters also demand intellectual property rights [copyrights, patents, etc.] that are highly protectionist. The World Trade Organization's version of patents (which today's rich countries would never have accepted while they were gaining their place in the sun) is not only extremely harmful to developing countries economically, but also undermines innovation—in fact, that's what they're *designed* to do. They call it "free trade," but what it really does is concentrate power.

The big transnationals want to reduce freedom by undermining the democratic functioning of the states in which they're based, while at the same time ensuring the government will be powerful enough to protect and support them. That's the essence of what I sometimes call "really existing market theory."

If you look through the whole history of modern economic development, you find that—virtually without exception—advocates of "free markets" want them applied to the poor and the middle-class but not to themselves. The government subsidizes corporations' costs, protects them from market risks and lets them keep the profits.

Can I smoke here in your office? If you deny me that, are you limiting my freedom?

I'm limiting your freedom but I'm increasing my rights. If you smoke in my office, it increases my chances of dying. Any effort to create a more human existence is going to inhibit somebody's freedom. If a kid crosses the street in front of me when I have a red light, that inhibits my freedom to run him over and get to work faster.

Public schools are another example. People who don't have children still have to pay school taxes, because we have a common feeling that it's good for our society if children are educated. Whether we personally have kids isn't relevant.

The most fanatic advocates of private despotism (who actually want to undermine freedom and democracy) naturally use nice words like *freedom*. What they really mean is that we have to have tyranny and a powerful state to ensure it. Just look at what they propose.

The Heritage Foundation, for instance, is full of talk about big philosophical issues, minimizing the state and so on, but they want to raise the Pentagon budget, because it's the major pipeline for public subsidy to high-tech industries. That's a hard line to defend, but as long as there isn't much in the way of intelligent public debate, they can get away with it.

The most extreme types, like Murray Rothbard, are at least honest. They'd like to eliminate highway taxes because they force you to pay for a road you may never drive on. As an alternative, they suggest that if you and I want to get somewhere, we should build a road there and then charge people tolls to go on it.

Just try generalizing that. Such a society couldn't survive, and even if it could, it would be so full of terror and hate that any human being would prefer to live in hell.

In any case, it's ridiculous to talk about freedom in a society dominated by huge corporations. What kind of freedom is there inside a corporation? They're totalitarian institutions—you take orders from above and maybe give them to people below you. There's about as much freedom as under Stalinism. Whatever rights workers have are guaranteed by the limited public authority that still exists.

When enormous, private, tyrannical institutions are granted the same rights as—or more rights than—human beings, freedom becomes something of a joke. The solution isn't to undermine freedom—it's to undermine the private tyrannies.

In Boulder [Colorado], where I live, an ordinance banning smoking in restaurants was put on the ballot. There was an enormous, well-funded campaign against it. Some city council members were threatened, and their actions were described as "fascist" and "Nazi-like." All in the name of freedom.

There's nothing new about that. In the past, the line was that Philip Morris has to be free to get twelve-year-old kids to smoke, and the kids' mothers are free to prevent them from smoking. Of course, Philip Morris has greater resources, and therefore more persuasive power, than thousands of parents and hundreds of city councils, but that was supposed to be irrelevant.

There was a funny coincidence a while back. The *New York Times* ran an op-ed by a senior fellow of the Hoover Institute about the "profound philosophical differences" that separate liberals and conservatives. The liberals want to see social policy administered at the federal level, while "conservatives prefer to transfer power to the states, in the belief that policies should be made closer to the people."

The same day, the *Wall Street Journal* ran a story headlined "What Fidelity Wants It Usually Gets, And It Wants Massachusetts Tax Cut." It opened by stating that "when Fidelity Investments talks, Massachusetts listens"—or else.

Massachusetts listens, the article explains, because Fidelity is one of the biggest firms in the state and can easily shift operations across the border to Rhode Island. That was exactly what it was threatening to do unless Massachusetts granted it "tax relief"—a subsidy, in effect, since "the people" pay more taxes to compensate for it. (New York recently had to do the same, when major financial firms threatened to move to New Jersey.) Massachusetts granted Fidelity the "relief."

A few months earlier, Raytheon had demanded tax and utility rate relief, perhaps to compensate for the fact that its shares had only about tripled in value in the past four years, while dividends per share rose 25% as well. The report on the business pages raised the (rhetorical) question whether Raytheon "is asking for tax dollars with one hand while passing money to shareholders with the other."

Again, Massachusetts listened to the threat to transfer out of state. Legislators had planned a big tax break for Massachusetts businesses generally, but restricted it to Raytheon and other "defense contractors."

It's an old story. Until the late 19th century, corporations were limited to functions explicitly determined by the state charters. That requirement effectively disappeared when New Jersey offered to drop it. Corporations began incorporating in New Jersey instead of New York, thus forcing New York to also drop the requirement and setting off a "race to the bottom."

The result was a substantial increase in the power of private tyrannies, providing them with new weapons to undermine liberty and human rights, and to administer markets in their own interest. The logic is the same when GM decides to invest in Poland, or when Daimler-Benz transfers production from Germany, where labor is highly paid, to Alabama, where it isn't.

By playing Alabama off against another competitor, North Carolina, Daimler-Benz received subsidies, protected markets and risk protection from "the people." (Smaller corporations can get into the act too, when states are forced to compete to bribe the powerful.)

Of course, it's far easier to play this game with states than countries. For Fidelity to move to Rhode Island, and for Raytheon to move to Tennessee, is no major problem—and Massachusetts knows it. Transferring operations overseas would be rather more difficult.

"Conservatives" are surely intelligent enough to understand that shifting decisions to the state level does not transfer power to "the people" but to those powerful enough to ask for subsidies with one hand and pocket them with the other. That's the "profound philosophical principle" that underlies the efforts of "conservatives" to shift power to the states.

There are still some defenses at the federal level, which is why it's been made the enemy (but not, of course, the parts that funnel money to large corporations—like the Pentagon, whose budget is going up, over the objections of more than 80% of the people).

According to a poll reported in the *Washington Post,* an enormous number of people think anything the federal government does is bad—except for the military, which we need (of course) to counter grave threats to US security. (Even so, people didn't want the military budget increased, as Clinton, Gingrich and the others proceeded to do.) *What could explain this?* the *Post* wondered.

Could it be fifty years of intense corporate propaganda, in the media and elsewhere, that have been trying to direct people's fear, anger and hatred against the government and make *private* power invisible to them? That isn't suggested as a reason. It's just a mystery why people have these strange ideas.

But there's no question they have them. When somebody wants to vent his anger at the fact that his life is falling apart, he's more likely to put a bomb in a federal building than in a corporate headquarters.

There are plenty of things wrong with government, but this propaganda opposes what's *right* with it—namely, that it's the one defense people have against private tyrannies.

To come back to the Boulder situation, is it an example of what you call "anti-politics"?

It's an example of opposition to democracy. It means that people shouldn't have a right to get together and democratically decide how they want to live.

You've frequently made the point that while corporate executives are getting everything they want on a silver platter, they're very leery of the far right, because they want to make sure their daughters continue to have access to abortion. But their daughters had access to abortions before Roe vs. Wade.

The executives don't want to have to do it secretly, and get involved in criminal activity. They want their wives and daughters to have normal freedoms and they want to live in a civilized society, not one in the grips of religious fundamentalism, where people around them think the world was created a couple of thousand years ago.

Another thing that worries them about this ultra-right tendency is that there's a populist streak in it. There's a lot of opposition to "bigness"—not just big government but big business too. The right wing doesn't see the point of things like funding for science, but business does, because it creates the technology and knowledge they'll exploit in the future.

Corporate executives also don't particularly like the idea of dismantling international institutions like the United Nations, or eliminating what's called foreign aid. They need those institutions, and they want them around. The jingoist, narrow-minded fanaticism that gave them deregulation, tort reform and the cutback of social services has another side to it, and they're definitely concerned about it.

ON THE HOME FRONT

THE MYTH OF HARD TIMES

When I called you the other day at home in Lexington, you were sitting in the dark, because the power had gone out.

I have a feeling we're going to be seeing more and more of that sort of thing. There simply hasn't been much investment in infrastructure. It's part of the drive for short-term profit: you let everything else go.

A lot of people are aware of it. We had a plumber in the other day, and he told us he had just bought himself a generator because he expects the power to be going off regularly.

Outsourcing is another aspect of it—it saves corporations' money today, but it destroys the potential work force. In the universities, they're hiring part-time junior faculty, who turn over fast. In research, there's a lot of pressure to do short-term, applied work, not the kind of basic, theoretical studies that were done in the 1950s and that laid the basis for the economy of today. The long-term effects of this are pretty obvious.

What do you think of this notion of scarcity—not enough jobs, not enough money, not enough opportunity?

Take a walk through any big city. Do you see anything that needs improvement?

There are huge amounts of work to be done, and lots of idle hands. People would be delighted to do the work, but the economic system is such a catastrophe it can't put them to work.

The country's awash in capital. Corporations have so much money they don't know what to do with it—it's coming out of their ears. There's no scarcity of funds—these aren't "lean and mean" times. That's just a fraud.

In 1996, President Clinton signed something called the Personal Responsibility and Work Opportunity Act, which eliminated the federal government's 61-year commitment to the poor. You've said that commitment was always very limited, and that it's declined sharply since about 1970.

When the assault began.

You've got to like the wording of that bill.

It says seven-year-old children have to take personal responsibility. It gives them opportunities they were deprived of before—like the opportunity to starve. It's just another assault against defenseless people, based on a very effective propaganda campaign to make people hate and fear the poor.

That's smart, because you don't want them looking at the *rich,* at what *Fortune* and *Business Week* call "dazzling" and "stupendous" profit growth, at the way the military system is pouring funds into advanced technology for the benefit of private industry. No, you want them to look at some imaginary black mother driving a Cadillac to pick up a welfare check so she can have more babies. *Why should I pay for that?* people ask.

The effectiveness of this campaign has been striking. Although most people think the government has a responsibility to ensure reasonable, minimal standards for poor people, they're also against welfare, which is what the government efforts to ensure reasonable, minimal standards for poor people are *called.* That's a propaganda achievement you have to admire.

There's another aspect of this that's much less discussed. One of the purposes of driving people away from welfare and into work is to lower wages by increasing the supply of workers.

The New York City government is now partially subsidizing workers driven out of the welfare system. The main effect has been to decrease unionized labor. Put a lot of unskilled labor into the workplace, make conditions so awful that people will take virtually any job, maybe throw in some public subsidy to keep them working, and you can drive down wages. It's a good way to make everybody suffer.

Ralph Nader calls the Republicans and the Democrats Tweedledum and Tweedledee.

There's never been much of a difference between the two business parties, but over the years, what differences there were have been disappearing.

In my view, the last liberal President was Richard Nixon. Since him, there've been nothing but conservatives (or what are called "conservatives"). The kind of gesture to liberalism that was required from the New Deal on became less necessary as new weapons of class war developed in the early '70s.

For the last twenty years, they've been used to bring about what the business press openly calls "capital's clear subjugation of labor." Under those circumstances, you can drop the liberal window-dressing.

Welfare capitalism was introduced in order to undercut democracy. If people are trying to take over some aspect of their lives and there doesn't seem any way to stop them, one standard historical response has been to say, *We rich folk will do it for you.* A classic example took place in Flint, Michigan, a town dominated by General Motors, around 1910.

There was a good deal of socialist labor organizing there, and plans had been developed to really take things over and provide more democratic public services. After some hesitation, the wealthy businessmen decided to go along with the progressive line. They said, *Everything you're saying is right, but we can do it a lot better, because we have all this money. You want a park? Fine. Vote for our candidate and he'll put in a park.*

Their resources undermined and eliminated the incipient democratic and popular structures. Their candidate won, and there was indeed welfare capitalism...until it wasn't needed any more, at which point it was dropped.

During the Depression, there was again a live union movement in Flint, and popular rights were again extended. But the business counterattack began right after the Second World War. It took a while this time, but by the '50s, it was getting somewhere.

It slowed somewhat in the sixties, when there was a lot more ferment—programs like the War on Poverty, things coming out of the civil rights movement—but by the early 1970s, it reached new heights, and it's been going pretty much full-steam ever since.

The typical picture painted by business propaganda since the Second World War—in everything from television comedies to scholarly books—has been: *We all live together in harmony. Joe Six-Pack, his loyal wife, the hard-working executive, the friendly banker—we're all one big happy family. We're all going to work together to defend ourselves against the bad guys out there—like union organizers and big government—who are trying to disrupt our harmony.* That's always the picture presented: class harmony between the people with the hammers and the people getting beaten over the head with them.

There's a campaign to undermine public confidence in Social Security, by saying it's going broke and that when the baby boomers reach retirement age, there'll be no money for them.

Most of the talk about Social Security is pretty fraudulent. Take the question of privatizing it. Social Security funds can be invested in the stock market whether the system is public or private. But putting people in charge of their own assets breaks down the solidarity that comes from doing something together, and diminishes the sense that people have any responsibility for each other.

Social Security says, *Let's ensure that all of us have a minimal standard of living.* That puts a bad idea into people's heads—that we can all work together, get involved in the democratic process and make our own decisions. Much better to create a world in which people behave individually and the powerful win.

The goal is a society in which the basic social unit is you and your television set. If the kid next door is hungry, it's not your problem. If the retired couple next door invested their assets badly and are now starving, that's not your problem either.

I think that's what lies behind the Social Security propaganda. The other issues are technical and probably not very significant. A slightly more progressive tax system could keep Social Security functioning for the indefinite future.

So we're moving from the idea that an injury to one is an injury to all, to the idea that an injury to one is just an injury to one.

That's the ideal of a capitalist society—except for the rich. Boards of directors are allowed to work together, and so are banks and investors and corporations in alliances with one another and with powerful states. That's fine. It's just the poor who aren't supposed to cooperate.

CORPORATE WELFARE

In an op-ed in the *Boston Globe,* Bernie Sanders of Vermont, the only Independent member of Congress, wrote, "If we're serious about balancing the budget in a fair way, we must slash corporate welfare." You've said you're very uncomfortable with the term *corporate welfare.* Why?

I like Bernie Sanders, and that was a good column, but I think he starts off on the wrong foot. Why should we balance the budget? Do you know a business—or a household—that doesn't have any debt?

I don't think we should balance the budget at all. The whole idea is just another weapon against social programs and in favor of the rich—in this case, mostly financial institutions, bondholders and the like.

Putting that aside, I don't hesitate to use the term *corporate welfare* because corporate welfare doesn't exist, or because it isn't a serious problem, but because people typically use the term to refer to specific government programs—a subsidy for ethanol manufacturers, say—rather than the more pervasive and fundamental ways government helps business. That's a serious error.

If it hadn't been for massive government interference, our automobile, steel and semiconductor industries probably wouldn't even exist today. The aerospace industry is even more thoroughly socialized. When Lockheed—Gingrich's favorite— was in big trouble back in the early 1970s, it was saved from destruction by a $250 million loan subsidized by the federal government. Same with Penn Central, Chrysler, Continental Illinois Bank and many others.

Right after the 1996 elections (I assume the timing wasn't accidental), the Clinton administration decided to funnel what's expected to amount to $750 *billion* or more of public money into developing new jet fighters, which we don't need for military purposes. The contract is to be awarded not to the traditional fighter manufacturer, Mc-Donnell Douglas, but to Lockheed Martin and/or Boeing, which hasn't produced a fighter plane for sixty years.

The reason is that Boeing sells commercial aircraft, our biggest civilian export. (The market for them is huge.) Commercial aircraft are often modified military aircraft, and adapt a lot of technology and design from them.

Boeing and McDonnell Douglas announced a merger, which was publicly subsidized to the tune of more than one billion dollars.

I'm sure the fact that McDonnell Douglas was knocked out of the competition for that fighter contract is part of the reason they're willing to be taken over by Boeing. In describing why Boeing was chosen over McDonnell Douglas, the Pentagon's undersecretary for acquisition and technology said, "We need to get hooks into the commercial research base to influence its growth." Defense Secretary William Perry explained that we've got to overcome earlier "barriers which limited timely access to rapidly evolving commercial technology."

"The Pentagon is ushering out the military-industrial complex and ushering in an industrial military complex," *NY Times* reporter Adam Bryant added, "noting that it's "not just an idle reordering of adjectives" but reflects Pentagon efforts "to do more business with companies that have a diverse customer base."

An aerospace industry analyst at Merrill Lynch pointed out that "this effort to broaden the industrial base that supports the military has been going on for a couple of years, but the Pentagon's decision [about the new Joint Strike fighter] was a major milestone in this trend."

In fact, "this effort" has been has going on not for "a couple of years" but for half a century, and its roots lie much deeper, in the crucial role of the military in developing the basic elements of the "American system of manufacturing" (standardization and interchangeable parts) in the 19th century.

In other words, a major purpose of military production and procurement, along with research and development in government labs or publicly funded private industry (by the Department of Energy and other agencies, as well as the Pentagon) is to subsidize private corporations. The public is simply being deluded about how they're paying for high technology.

By now this stuff is described almost openly—usually on the business pages but sometimes even on the front page. That's one of the nice things about the end of the Cold War—the clouds lift a bit. More people now realize, at least to some extent, that the military system has been partially a scam, a cover for ensuring that advanced sectors of industry can continue to function at public expense. This is part of the underpinnings of the whole economic system, but it's off the agenda when most people talk about corporate welfare.

I'm not saying public financing shouldn't exist, by the way. I think it's a very good idea to fund research in the science and technology of the future. But there are two small problems: public funding shouldn't be funneled through private tyrannies (let alone the military system), and the public should decide what to invest in. I don't think we should live in a society where the rich and powerful determine how public money is spent, and nobody even knows about their decisions.

Ironically, the politicians who prate the most about minimizing government are exactly the ones most likely to expand its business-funding role. The Reagan administration poured money into advanced technology and was the most protectionist in postwar American history. Reagan probably didn't know what was going on, but the people around him virtually doubled various import restrictions. His Treasury secretary, James Baker, boasted that they'd raised tariffs higher than any postwar government.

Government subsidies to private industry are unusually large here, but they exist in all the industrial nations. The Swedish economy, for instance, rests heavily on big transnational corporations—weapons manufacturers, in particular. Sweden's military industry appears to have provided much of the technology that allowed Ericsson to carve out a large share of the mobile phone market.

Meanwhile, the Swedish welfare state is being cut back. It's still way better than ours, but it's being reduced—while the multinationals' profits increase.

Business wants the popular aspects of government, the ones that actually serve the population, beaten down, but it also wants a very powerful state, one that works for it and is removed from public control.

Do you think corporate welfare is a good wedge issue to get people involved in politics?

I'm not a great tactician, and maybe this is a good way to stir people up, but I think it would be better for them to think through the issues and figure out the truth. Then they'll stir themselves up.

CRIME: SUITES VS. STREETS

The media pays a lot of attention to crime in the streets, which the FBI estimates costs about $4 billion a year. The *Multinational Monitor* estimates that white-collar crime—what Ralph Nader calls "crime in the suites"—costs about $200 billion a year. That generally gets ignored.

Although crime in the US is high by the standards of comparable societies, there's only one major domain in which it's really off the map—murders with guns. But that's because of the gun culture. The overall crime rate hasn't changed much for a long time. In fact, it's been decreasing recently.

The US is one of very few societies—maybe the only one—where crime is considered a political issue; in most parts of the world, it's looked at as a social problem. Politicians don't have to fight during elections about who's tougher on crime—they simply try to figure out how to deal with it.

Why does crime get all this attention here? I think it has more to do with social control than with crime itself. There's a very committed effort to convert the US into something resembling a Third World society, where a few people have enormous wealth and a lot of others have no security (for one reason, because their jobs might be sent to Mexico or some other place where employers don't have to worry about benefits, unions or the like).

Now that these workers are superfluous, what do you do with them? First of all, you have to make sure they don't notice that society is unfair and try to change that, and the best way to distract them is to get them to hate and fear one another. Every coercive society immediately hits on that idea, which has two other benefits: it reduces the number of superfluous people (by violence) and provides places to put the ones who survive (prisons).

The utterly fraudulent war on drugs was undertaken at a time when everyone knew that the use of every drug—even coffee—was falling among educated whites, and was staying sort of level among blacks. The police obviously find it much easier to make an arrest on the streets of a black ghetto than in a white suburb. By now, a very high percentage of incarceration is drug-related, and it mostly targets little guys, somebody who's caught peddling dope.

The big guys are largely ignored. The US Department of Commerce publishes regular data on foreign operations of US business (estimates only, with delays; the details are unknown). In late 1996 it reported that in 1993–95, about a quarter of direct foreign investment in the Western Hemisphere (apart from Canada) was in Bermuda.

The figures for majority-owned foreign affiliates of US corporations (other than banks) were about a quarter in Bermuda and another 15% in Panama, the British Caribbean islands and other tax havens. Most of the rest seems to be short-term speculative money—picking up assets in, say, Brazil.

Now, they're not building manufacturing plants in Bermuda. The most benign interpretation is that it's some form of tax evasion. Quite possibly it's narco-capital. The OECD [the Organization of Economic Cooperation and Development, a Paris-based group representing the 29 richest nations] estimates that more than half of all narco-money— something like $250 *billion*—goes through US banks each year. But, as far as I know, nobody's looking into this dirty money.

It's also been known for years that American industrial producers have been sending way more of the chemicals used in drug production to Latin America than there's any conceivable legal use for. This has occasionally led to executive orders requiring the manufacturers to monitor what chemicals they sell to whom, but I haven't seen any prosecutions on this.

Corporate crime isn't just ignored in the area of drugs. Take what happened with the S&Ls. Only a very small part of it was treated as crime; most of it was just picked up by the taxpayer with bailouts. Is that surprising? Why should rich and powerful people allow themselves to be prosecuted?

Russell Mokhiber of the *Corporate Crime Reporter* contrasts two statistics: 24,000 Americans are murdered each year, while 56,000 Americans die from job-related accidents and diseases.

That's another example of unpunished corporate crime. In the '80s, the Reagan administration essentially informed the business world that it was not going to prosecute violations of OSHA [Occupational Safety and Health Administration] regulations. As a result, the number of industrial accidents went up rather dramatically. *Business Week* reported that working days lost to injury almost doubled from 1983 to 1986, in part because "under Reagan and Bush" OSHA "was a hands-off agency."

The same is true of the environmental issues—toxic waste disposal, say. Sure, they're killing people, but is it criminal? Well, it *should* be.

Howard Zinn and I visited a brand-new maximum-security federal prison in Florence, Colorado. The lobby has high ceilings, tile floors, glass everywhere. Around the same time, I read that New York City schools are so overcrowded that students are meeting in cafeterias, gyms and locker rooms. I found that quite a juxtaposition.

They're certainly related. Both prisons and inner-city schools target a kind of superfluous population that there's no point educating because there's nothing for them to do. Because we're a civilized people, we put them in prison, rather than sending death squads out to murder them.

Drug-related crimes, usually pretty trivial ones, are mostly what's filling up the prisons. I haven't seen many bankers or executives of chemical corporations in prison. People in the rich suburbs commit plenty of crimes, but they're not going to prison at anything like the rate of the poor.

There's another factor too. Prison construction is by now a fairly substantial part of the economy. It's not yet on the scale of the Pentagon, but for some years now it's been growing fast enough to get the attention of big financial institutions like Merrill Lynch, who have been floating bonds for prison construction.

High-tech industry, which has been feeding off the Pentagon for research and development, is turning to the idea of administering prisons with supercomputers, surveillance technology, etc. In fact, I wouldn't be entirely surprised to see fewer people in prisons and more people imprisoned in their homes. It's probably within reach of the new technology to have surveillance devices that control people wherever they are. So if you pick up the telephone to make a call they don't like, alarms go off or you get a shock.

It saves the cost of building prisons. That hurts the construction industry, true, but it contributes to the high-tech sector, which is the more advanced, growing, dynamic part of the economy.

It sounds like an Orwellian *1984* scenario you're describing.

Call it Orwellian or whatever you like—I'd say it's just ordinary state capitalism. It's a natural evolution of a system that subsidizes industrial development and seeks to maximize short-term profit for the few at the cost of the many.

If you'd predicted, thirty or forty years ago, that there'd be smoke-free flights and restaurants, and that the tobacco companies would be under intense attack, no one would have believed you.

Through the 1980s, the use of all substances—drugs, smoking, coffee, etc.—declined, by and large, among the more educated and wealthier sectors of the population. Because the cigarette companies know they're going to end up losing that portion of their market, they've been expanding rapidly into foreign markets, which are forced open by US government power.

You still find plenty of poor, uneducated people smoking; in fact, tobacco has become such a lower-class drug that some legal historians are predicting that it will become illegal. Over the centuries, when some substance became associated with "the dangerous classes," it's often been outlawed. Prohibition of alcohol in this country was, in part, aimed at working-class people in New York City saloons and the like. The rich kept drinking as much as they wanted.

I'm not in favor of smoking being made illegal, by the way, any more than I'm in favor of making other class-related substances illegal. But it's a murderous habit that kills huge numbers of people and harms plenty of others, so the fact that it's come under some sort of control is a step forward.

In August 1996, Gary Webb wrote a three-part article in the *San Jose Mercury News,* which was expanded

39

into a book called *Dark Alliance*. Webb alleged that the CIA had been making money selling crack cocaine in the black ghetto in Los Angeles, and in fact was responsible for the explosion of that drug's popularity in the 1980s.

I've noticed that you tend to stay away from such stories—at least until you're asked about them during a question-and-answer period. You don't devote much energy to them.

I just look at them differently. The Webb story is fundamentally correct, but the fact that the CIA has been involved in drug-running has been well-known since Al McCoy's work 25 years ago. It started right after the Second World War. You can follow the trail through the French connection in Marseilles (a consequence of CIA efforts to undermine unions by reconstituting the Mafia for strike-breaking and disruption), to the Golden Triangle in Laos and Burma, and on to Afghanistan, etc.

Bob Parry and Brian Barger exposed a lot of the story ten years ago. Their evidence was correct, but they were shut up very quickly. Webb's contribution was to trace some of the details and discover that cocaine got into the ghettos by a particular pathway.

When the CIA says they didn't know anything about it, I assume they're right. Why should they want to know anything about details like that? That it's going to end up in the ghettos isn't a plot—it's just going to happen in the natural course of events. It's not going to sneak into well-defended communities that can protect themselves. It's going to break into devastated communities where people have to fight for survival, where kids aren't cared for because their parents are working to put food on the table.

So of course there's a connection between the CIA and drugs. The US was involved in massive international terrorism throughout Central America. It was mostly clandestine (which means people in powerful positions in government and the media knew about it, but it was enough below the surface that they could pretend they didn't). To get untraceable money and brutal thugs, our government naturally turned to narco-traffickers— like Noriega (he was our great friend, remember, until he became too independent). None of this is a secret or a surprise.

Where I differ from a lot of other people is, I don't think the CIA has been involved as an inde- pendent agency: I think it does what it's told to do by the White House. It's used as an instrument of state policy, to carry out operations the govern- ment wants to be able to "plausibly deny."

THE MEDIA

In *Manufacturing Consent,* the book you wrote with Ed Herman in 1988, you described five filters that news goes through before we see it. Would you revise that list? One of the filters, anticommunism, probably needs to be changed.

Temporarily, at least. I thought at the time it was put too narrowly. More broadly, it's the idea that grave enemies are about to attack us and we need to huddle under the protection of domestic power.

You need something to frighten people with, to prevent them from paying attention to what's really happening to them. You have to somehow engender fear and hatred, to channel the kind of rage—or even just discontent—that's being aroused by social and economic conditions.

By the early '80s, it was clear that Communism wasn't going to remain usable as a threat for much longer, so when the Reagan administration came in, they immediately focussed on "international terrorism." Right from the start, they used Libya as a punching bag.

Then every time they had to rally support for aid to the Contras or something, they'd engineer a confrontation with Libya. It got so ludicrous that, at one point, the White House was surrounded with tanks to protect poor President Reagan from Libyan hit squads. It became an international joke.

By the late '80s, Hispanic drug traffickers became the enemy; by now, they've been joined by immigrants, black criminals, welfare mothers and a whole host of other attackers on every side.

Toward the end of *Manufacturing Consent,* you conclude that "the societal purpose of the media is to...defend the economic, social and political agenda of privileged groups that dominate the domestic society and the state." Anything you'd want to add to that?

It's such a truism that it's almost unnecessary to put it into words. It would be amazing if that *weren't* true. Assuming virtually nothing except that there's a free market—or something resembling one—virtually forces you to that conclusion.

In *Z* magazine, Ed Herman discussed the persistence of the idea that the media are liberal.

Ed's main point is perfectly valid—what really matters is the desires of the people who own and control the media. But I may slightly disagree with him about whether they're liberal. In my view, national media like the *Washington Post* and the *New York Times* probably meet the current definition of the word *liberal*. Sometimes they even run things I approve of.

For instance, to my amazement, the *New York Times* actually had an editorial in favor of greater workers' rights in Indonesia (as opposed to the right-wing view that it's OK to strangle Indonesian workers if you can make more money that way). The *Times* also has columnists—Bob Herbert is one example—that I don't think you would have seen there forty years ago, and they often write very good stuff.

But in general, the mainstream media all make certain basic assumptions, like the necessity of maintaining a welfare state for the rich. Within that framework, there's some room for differences of opinion, and it's entirely possible that the major media are toward the liberal end of that range. In fact, in a well-designed propaganda system, that's exactly where they should be.

The smart way to keep people passive and obedient is to strictly limit the spectrum of acceptable opinion, but allow very lively debate within that spectrum—even encourage the more critical and dissident views. That gives people the sense that there's free thinking going on, while all the time the presuppositions of the system are being reinforced by the limits put on the range of the debate.

So you're allowed to discuss whether the Mideast "peace process" should be implemented immediately or should be delayed, and whether Israel is sacrificing too much or just the right amount. But you're not allowed to discuss the fact—and it certainly is a fact—that this so-called "peace process" wiped out a 25-year, internationally supported diplomatic effort recognizing the national rights of both contending parties, and rammed home the US position that denies these rights to the Palestinians.

Let's clarify what it really means to say the media are liberal. Suppose 80% of all journalists vote Democratic. Does that mean they're liberal in any meaningful sense of the word, or just that they're at the left end of an extremely narrow, center-right spectrum? (Most of my writing has been a criticism of the liberal end of the media, the ones who set the leftmost boundary for acceptable opinion.)

Take it a step further. Suppose it turns out that 80% of all journalists are flaming radicals who'd really rather be writing for Z. Would that show that the media themselves are radical? Only if you assume that the media are open to the free expression of ideas (by their reporters, in this case).

But that's exactly the thesis under debate, and you can't establish it by presupposing it. The empirical evidence that this thesis is false is overwhelming, and there has been no serious attempt to address it. Instead, it's just *assumed* that the media are open. It's possible to get away with that kind of thinking if power is sufficiently concentrated and educated sections of the population are sufficiently obedient.

The University of Illinois Press has published a US edition of *Taking the Risk out of Democracy* by the noted Australian scholar Alex Carey. One of the chapters is entitled *Grassroots and Treetops Propaganda.* What does Carey mean by that?

Treetops propaganda is the kind of thing that Ed Herman and I are mostly commenting on. It's the elite media, aimed at educated sectors of the population that are more involved in decision-making and setting a general framework and agenda for others to adhere to. Grassroots propaganda is aimed at the vulgar masses, to keep them distracted and out of our hair, and to make sure they don't interfere in the public arena, where they don't belong.

Do you find it ironic that one of the major works on US propaganda is written by an Australian?

Not at all. Alex Carey was an old friend; in fact, we dedicated *Manufacturing Consent* to him. He really pioneered the study of corporate propaganda, of which the media is just one aspect. He was working on a big book on the subject, but he died before it was completed.

Although corporate propaganda is a major force in contemporary history, it's very little studied, because people aren't supposed to know that major corporations are deeply dedicated to controlling the public mind, and have been for a long time. Carey quotes the business press as saying that the public mind is the greatest "hazard facing industrialists."

We're supposed to believe that the press is liberal, dangerous, adversarial, out of control. That itself is an extremely good example of corporate propaganda.

More than 700 people died in a Chicago heat wave in the summer of 1995. They were mostly old people living in poor neighborhoods who couldn't afford air conditioning. I think the headlines should have read, *Market Kills 700.*

You're absolutely right—honest media would have reported how the workings of the market system added more deaths to the toll. Every story in the paper could be recast with a more honest and humane point of view, one not reflecting the interests of the powerful. But expecting them to do that on their own initiative is like expecting General Motors to give away its profits to poor people in the slums.

Anthony Lewis, someone you often identified as the outer liberal fringe allowed in the *Times,* celebrated the *Pentagon Papers* on their 25th anniversary as a great example of media heroism and courage. He wrote that "we were a much tamer press before 1971."

There's been a bit of a change. The 1960s opened up society in many ways, from personal attitudes to dress codes to beliefs. That affected everything, including corporations and the corporate media—which now are, in many respects, less automatically disciplined than they were back in the sixties.

There was a column around the same time by Randolph Ryan. He's someone who came out of the '60s and did extremely good reporting on Central America for the *Boston Globe* in the '80s. The '60s culture also affected the *Globe*'s editor, Tom Winship—whose son was a draft resister, incidentally. What was happening influenced his thinking and improved the newspaper in lots of ways. So sure, the '60s had a big effect. But the publication of the *Pentagon Papers* in 1971 wasn't really part of it.

In 1968, after the Tet offensive [a massive assault by the southern resistance (called the "Viet Cong" by the US) with the support of North Vietnamese troops, during the Vietnamese holiday of Tet], corporate America basically decided that the war wasn't worth it. They came to believe that we'd essentially achieved what we needed to, and that continuing was just too costly. So they told Johnson to enter into some form of negotiations and to start withdrawing American troops.

It wasn't until about a year and a half later that the media here began to respond to the opening that corporate America had left for them by voicing very timid criticisms of the war. As I recall, the first newspaper to call for American withdrawal from Vietnam was the *Boston Globe*.

It was around then that Lewis started saying that the war began with "blundering efforts to do good" but that by 1969(!) it had become clear that it was "a disastrous mistake" and that the US "could not impose a solution except at a price too costly to itself." (By the same token, *Pravda* was probably saying, around 1980 or 1981, *The war in Afghanistan began with blundering efforts to do good, but now it's clear that it's a disastrous mistake and too costly for Russia.)*

Of course, Vietnam wasn't a "disastrous mistake"—it was murderous aggression. When the *Times* starts writing *that,* we'll know something has changed.

Most of the important parts of the *Pentagon Papers* never appeared in the *Times* and haven't been discussed in the mainstream literature either. The parts the *Times did* publish weren't all that revealing. Although they contained some new information, for the most part they simply confirmed what was already available in the public record. The *Times'* willingness to publish them, three years after the main centers of American power had decided the war should be ended, wasn't exactly an act of enormous heroism.

Because the government is giving less funding to public radio and TV, they're being forced more and more to turn to corporate funding.

Public radio and TV have always been very marginal enterprises. As Bob McChesney describes, there was a struggle back in the '20s and '30s over whether radio should be in the public arena or handed over to private power. You know which side won. When television came along, there wasn't even much of a debate—it was just given to business.

Both times this was done in the name of democracy! It tells you what a strange intellectual culture this is—we take the media out of the hands of the public, give them to private tyrannies, and call it *democracy.*

Over time, this attitude has solidified. The 1996 Telecommunications Act was the biggest give-away of public assets in history. Even token payments weren't required.

McChesney makes the interesting and important point that this wasn't treated as a social and political issue—you read about it in the business pages, not on the front page. The issue of *whether* we should give away these public resources to private power wasn't discussed—just *how* we should give them away. That was a tremendous propaganda victory.

Public radio and television are permitted around the fringes, partly because the commercial media were criticized for not fulfilling the public-interest duties required of them by law. So they said, *Let the public stations take care of that. Let them run Hamlet.* Now, even that marginal function is being narrowed.

This doesn't necessarily mean the death of public radio and television, by the way. Back in the Middle Ages, the arts were supported almost entirely by benevolent autocrats like the Medicis; maybe today's benevolent autocrats will do the same. After all, they're the ones who support the operas and symphonies.

McChesney also notes that most broadcast innovation has taken place in public radio and television, not commercial. FM radio was public until it started making money, then it became private. The Internet is a dramatic example today—it's designed, funded and run in the public sector as long as you can't make money on it, but as soon as it shows a potential for profitability, it's handed over to megacorporations.

Two Academy Award-winning documentaries, Deadly Deception *(about General Electric) and* The Panama Deception, *and a film about you,* Manufacturing Consent, *were hardly shown on public TV.*

Things used to be even worse. I spent a couple of weeks in Indochina in early 1970. At that point I was pretty well known in the Boston area, which is home to NPR's flagship affliliate, WGBH. With great reluctance, WGBH's big liberal leader, Louis M. Lyons, agreed to interview me—extremely hostilely—for a few minutes. That was probably the only time I was on local public radio back then.

I'm not a great admirer of today's media, but I think they're way better and more open than they were thirty or forty years ago. People who went through the '60s are now in the media and are writing—at least partially—from more humane points of view.

What would the media look like in a genuinely democratic society?

They'd be under public control. Their design, the material they present, access to them, would all be the result of public participation—at least to the extent that people want to be involved, and I think they would.

Some of the media in this country were once more democratic. Not to be too exotic, let's go back to the 1950s, when eight hundred labor newspapers, reaching twenty or thirty million people a week, were devoted to struggling against the commercial press, which was "damning labor at every opportunity," as they put it, and "selling" the "virtues of big business"—driving the mythology into people's heads.

Bob McChesney says that in the early '40s, there were about a thousand labor-beat reporters. Today there are seven.

Every newspaper has a business section, which responds to the interests of a small part of the population—the part that happens to control the newspaper, oddly enough. But I've never seen a labor section in a newspaper. When labor news is run at all, it's in the business section, and is looked at from that point of view. This simply reflects, in a very transparent way, who's in power.

Lots of people criticize the ongoing tabloidization of the news. The program directors respond by saying, *We're giving the public what it wants. No one's forcing them to turn on the TV and watch our program.* What do you think about that?

First of all, I don't agree that that's what the public wants. To take just one example, I think people in New York would have been interested in learning that NAFTA was expected to harm "women, blacks and hispanics" and "semi-skilled production workers" (70% of all workers are categorized as "semi-skilled")—as the very careful reader of the *Times* could discover the day *after* Congress passed NAFTA.

Even then, the facts were concealed in an upbeat story about the likely winners: "the region's banking, telecommunications and service firms, from management consultants and public relations to law and marketing," "banks and Wall

Street securities firms," the capital-intensive chemical industry, publishing (including media corporations), etc.

But that aside, what people want is in part socially created—it depends on what sort of experiences they've had in their lives, and what sort of opportunities. Change the structure and they'll choose different things.

I visited a working-class slum in Brazil where people gather during prime television time to watch locally produced films on a large outdoor screen. They prefer them to the soap operas and other junk on commercial TV, but they can only have that preference because they were offered the choice.

When people in the US are surveyed, it turns out that what they want—overwhelmingly—is commercial-free television. Do you see commercial-free television? Of course not. In US television, big corporations sell audiences to other businesses, and they're not interested in providing us with other options.

In an article titled *The Strange Disappearance of Civic America,* Robert Putnam named TV as the culprit.

Putnam is a sociologist at Harvard who's quite mainstream. He found about a 50% decline since the 1960s in *any* form of interaction—visiting a neighbor, going to PTA meetings, joining a bowling league. One reason children watch so much TV is that parent-child interaction has dropped 40% or so from the '60s to today—at least in part because both parents have to work fifty hours a week to put food on the table. There's little day care and few support systems available, so what are you left with? TV baby-sitting.

But it's a little thin to blame TV itself. It isn't a force of nature—it's the core of the marketing culture, and it's designed to have certain effects. It's not trying to empower you. You don't find messages on TV about how to join a union and do something about the conditions of your life. Over and over again, it rams into your head messages designed to destroy your mind and separate you from other people. That eventually has an effect.

What's happening with TV is part of something much broader. Elites always regard democracy as a major threat, something to be defended against. It's been well understood for a long time that the best defense against democracy is to distract people. That's why 19th-century businessmen sponsored evangelical religion, people talking in tongues, etc.

Kids are watching TV forty hours a week. It's a form of pacification.

It is a kind of pacification program.

MORE MONEY, FEWER VOTERS

Clinton said the 1996 elections were a vindication of "the vital center," which he locates somewhere between "overheated liberalism and chilly conservatism." What was your reading of these elections?

Was there any choice other than "the vital center"? Clinton and Dole behaved slightly differently, and had somewhat different constituencies, but both were moderate Republicans, old-time government insiders and more or less inter-changeable representatives of the business com-munity.

I think the election was a vote *against* the vital center. Both candidates were unpopular and very few people expected anything from either one of them. Voter turnout was *49%*—as low as it's ever been—and I think that reflected the general feel-ing that the political system isn't functioning.

I thought the turnout was the lowest since 1924.

1924 is misleading, because it was the first year women were allowed to vote. A smaller percentage of the electorate voted simply because a lot of women weren't used to voting and didn't do it the first time around. If you take that into account, 1996 may have been the lowest voter turnout ever.

The 1996 campaign also cost the most ever—$1.6 bil-lion that we know about. More and more money is being spent, and fewer and fewer people are voting.

As one of the television commentators pointed out, these weren't conventions—they were coro-nations. It's just another step towards eliminating whatever functioning elements remain in formal democracy, and is all part of the general business attack on freedom, markets and democracy.

Compare Haiti, the poorest country in the hemi-sphere. The creation of a vibrant, lively, indepen-dent, civil society there during the last few years has been remarkable, and was the basis for a remarkable triumph of democracy (which was extinguished very quickly and brutally with US help, and in a way that bars its revival).

If there were an independent intelligentsia in the US, they'd be falling off their chairs laughing at the idea that we have something to teach Haiti about democracy. Civil society is collapsing here. We have to go *there* to learn something about democracy.

Another commentator compared elections to auctions, with the prize going to the highest bidder.

They've never been much different from that, but yes, they're getting worse. On the other hand, if the public responds—if, for example, union organizing increases and grassroots organizations develop—things will change. The first change will be the political establishment saying, *Okay, we'll be more benevolent autocrats.* If they're pressured beyond that, we can get significant social change.

Most people realize that the political parties don't care about them. Public disaffection is enormous, but it's mostly directed against government. That's because business propaganda, which dominates the media, directs it that way. There may also be a lot of disaffection with business, but we don't really know, since that kind of question isn't asked much in the polls.

What's your take on campaign finance reform?

It's not a bad thing, but it's not going to have much effect. There are too many ways to cheat. It's like pretending to try to stop drug importation. There are so many ways to bring drugs in that there's no stopping them.

The real problem isn't campaign financing—it's the overwhelming power corporate tyrannies wield. Campaign finance reform isn't going to change that.

IS CORPORATE POWER INVINCIBLE?

Let me run a couple of quotes by you. The first is from Robert Reich, Clinton's former secretary of labor: "The jury is still out on whether the traditional union is necessary for the new workplace." The second is from Clinton's former commerce secretary, the late Ron Brown: "Unions are OK where they are, and where they're not, it's not clear yet what sort of organization should represent workers."

I think that's not surprising, coming from a moderate Republican administration. Why let working people have ways to defend themselves against private power?

Maybe something else is needed in the high-tech workplace—"flexibility," which is a fancy way of saying that when you go to sleep at night, you don't know if you'll have a job in the morning (but you *do* know you won't have benefits). "Flexibility" is terrific for profits, but it destroys human beings.

There was a famous quote—at it least it should be famous—by a Brazilian general (around 1970, I think). Speaking of the Brazilian "economic miracle," he said that the economy is doing fine— it's just the people that aren't. That pretty much says it all.

Something about this puzzles me. It's in corporations' interest to make sure consumers have enough money to buy their products. This was the logic behind Henry Ford's raising his workers' pay to $5 a day, so that they could afford to buy the cars they were building.

It's in your interest to make profit, but there are other ways to do it than by selling a large quantity of goods to a mass market that's partially made up of your own workers. Maybe it's more in your interest to use extremely cheap, oppressed labor to produce fewer goods for relatively wealthy people, while at the same time making money through financial speculation.

When the managers of transnational corporations are asked about the very low wages they pay their workers in the Third World, they say, *These people didn't have a job before, we're giving them work, they're learning a trade,* and so on. How would you respond to that?

If they're serious about that, they would use some of their profits to support better working conditions in Indonesia. How often do they do that? They're not short of money—just read the *Fortune* 500 reports every year.

By the way, I'm not criticizing corporate executives individually. If one of them tried to use corporate funds to improve working conditions in Indonesia, he'd be out on his ear in three seconds. In fact, it would probably be illegal.

A corporate executive's responsibility is to his stockholders—to maximize profit, market share and power. If he can do that by paying starvation wages to women who'll die in a couple of years because their working conditions are so horrible, he's just doing his job. It's the *job* that should be questioned.

Aren't corporate managers quick to adjust and make small concessions, like letting people go the bathroom twice a day instead of once?

Absolutely. The same was true of kings and princes—they made plenty of concessions when they weren't able to control their subjects. The same was true of slave owners.

Small concessions are all to the good. People in the Third World may suffer a little less, and people here may see that activism can work, which will inspire them to push farther. Both are good outcomes. Eventually you get to the point where you start asking, *Why should we be asking them to make concessions? Why are they in power in the first place? What do we need the king for?*

I was recently in Trinidad, which is under "structural adjustment." While talking to some laborers, I asked them how they got to their job site. They said they had to take a taxi. I asked, *Isn't there any bus service?* and they told me that the route from the poor part of Port of Spain where they lived had been eliminated, and they now had to pay a substantial part of their earnings on private taxis.

It's happening everywhere. Transferring costs from the rich to the poor is the standard device of improving "efficiency."

I drove to work this morning. The roads are full of potholes, and there were big traffic jams, but it's hard to use public transportation, because it takes too long and is, in fact, more expensive than driving.

Depriving people of an alternative to driving forces them to buy more cars and more gas. Potholes increase car repairs and purchases. More driving increases pollution, and dealing with the health effects of that pollution costs even more money.

All the discomfort of all these people increases the gross national product (allowing celebration of the great economy) and is highly efficient from the point of view of the corporations who own the place. The costs that are transferred to the public, like the taxi fares those poor workers in Trinidad have to pay, aren't measured.

Los Angeles had a very extensive public transportation network that was simply bought up destroyed.

Yes, and the same was true around here. Earlier in this century, you could get all around New England via electric railways.

Why do we have a society where everyone has to drive a car, live out in the suburbs, go to big shopping malls? In the 1950s, the government began a huge highway construction program called the National Defense Highway System. They had to put in the word *Defense* to justify the huge sums they were pouring into it, but in effect, it was a way of shifting from public transportation like railroads to a system that would use more automobiles, trucks, gasoline and tires (or airplanes).

It was part of one of the biggest social engineering projects in history, and it was initiated by a true conspiracy. General Motors, Firestone Tire and Standard Oil of California (Chevron) simply bought up and destroyed the public transportation system in Los Angeles, in order to force people to use their products.

The issue went to court, the corporations were fined a few thousand dollars, and then the government took over the whole process. The same happened elsewhere. State and local governments also joined in, and a wide range of business power. It's had enormous effects, and it certainly didn't happen by market principles.

It's still happening. One new plan in Boston is to dismantle parts of the public transportation system and privatize them—to make them more "efficient" (they claim) by letting private tyrannies run them. It's obvious what they'll do. If you're head of a corporation that runs the transportation system and your responsibility is to make sure your stockholders make money, what would you do? Cut off unprofitable routes, get rid of unions, etc.

There's quite a bit of activism against sweatshops that profit transnationals like The Gap, Disney, Nike, Reebok, etc. Do you think these campaigns are getting to systemic issues?

I think they're really good campaigns. To ask whether they're getting to systemic issues is, I think, misleading—the kind of question that undermined a lot of traditional Marxist politics.

Systemic questions grow out of people learning more and more about how the world works, step-by-step. If you become aware that people in Haiti are being paid a couple of cents an hour to make money for rich people here, that ultimately—and maybe a lot sooner than ultimately—leads to questions about the structure of power in general.

The current economic system appears to be triumphant, but you've said that it's going to self-destruct—that that's inherent in its logic. Do you still feel that way?

I actually said something different. The current system has elements in it that look like they're going to self-destruct. But it's unclear whether the whole world is going to turn into something like a Third World country where wealth is highly concentrated, resources are used to protect the wealthy, and the general public finds itself somewhere between unpleasantness and actual misery.

I don't think that kind of world can survive very long, but I can't prove it. It's kind of an experiment. Nobody knows the answer, because nobody understands these things well enough.

Opinion polls show how much people dislike this system. When *Business Week* surveyed public attitudes towards business, they were pretty startled by the results. 95% of the people—there's a number you almost never see in a poll—said corporations have a responsibility to reduce profit for the benefit of their workers and the communities they do business in. 70% thought businesses have too much power, and roughly the same number thought business has gained more by deregulation and similar measures than the general population has.

Other studies taken around the same time show that over 80% of the population think that working people don't have enough say in what goes on, that the economic system is inherently unfair, and that the government basically isn't functioning, because it's working for the rich.

The poll questions still fall way short of what working people in eastern Massachusetts (and elsewhere) were asking for about 150 years ago. They weren't saying, *Be a little more benevolent. Give us few scraps.* They were saying, *You have no right to rule. We should own the factories. The people who work in the mills ought to own them.*

Many people today just want business to be a bit nicer, for there to be a little less corporate welfare and a little more welfare capitalism. But others would like to see more radical changes; we don't know how many, because the polls don't ask about radical alternatives, and they aren't readily available for people to think about.

People are tremendously cynical about institutions. A lot of this cynicism takes very antisocial and irrational forms, and the amount of propaganda and manipulation is so enormous that most people don't see alternatives, but the attitudes that might lead to acceptance—even enthusiastic acceptance—of alternatives are just below the surface.

You can see it in their actions—both destructive, like selling drugs in the streets, and constructive, like the strikes in South Korea. What South Korean workers consider totally intolerable is the idea that private power should have the right to replace strikers with permanent replacement workers. And they're right—that's against international labor standards.

There *is* a country that's been censured by the International Labor Organization for carrying out those practices—the US. That tells us something about who's civilized and who isn't.

People concerned about corporate power and its excesses are urged to invest in "socially responsible businesses." What do you think of that?

I have no criticism of that idea, but people shouldn't have any illusions about it. It's like preferring benevolent autocrats to murderous ones. Sometimes you get a benevolent ruler, but he can always stop being benevolent whenever he feels like it. Sure, I'd rather have an autocrat who doesn't go around torturing children, but it's the autocracy itself that needs to be eliminated.

Richard Grossman, Ward Morehouse and others have been advocating the revocation of corporate charters [the documents that create corporations and allow them to conduct business]. I'm wondering how realistic this is. This would have to happen in state legislatures, which are almost entirely under the control of big business.

I certainly think people should begin to question the legitimacy of corporate institutions. In their current form, they're a rather recent phenomenon; their rights were created, mostly by the judicial system, in the late 1800s and were dramatically expanded early in this century.

In my view, corporations are illegitimate institutions of tyrannical power, with intellectual roots not unlike those of fascism and Bolshevism. (There was a time when that kind of analysis wasn't uncommon—for example, in the work of political economist Robert Brady over fifty years ago. It has very deep roots in working-class movements, Enlightenment thought and classical liberalism.)

There are, as you point out, legal mechanisms for dissolving corporations, since they all have to have state charters. But let's not delude ourselves—these are massive changes. Just suggesting charter revocation as a tactic doesn't make any sense—it can only be considered after legislatures reflect the public interest instead of business interests, and that will require very substantial education and organization, and construction of alternative institutions to run the economy more democratically.

But we can—and should—certainly begin pointing out that corporations are fundamentally illegitimate, and that they don't have to exist at all in their modern form. Just as other oppressive institutions—slavery, say, or royalty—have been changed or eliminated, so corporate power can be changed or eliminated. What are the limits? There aren't any. Everything is ultimately under public control.

AROUND THE WORLD

IS GLOBALIZATION INEVITABLE?

Germany has unemployment levels not seen there since 1933. Companies like Siemens and Bosch are closing down their German factories and moving overseas. You've commented on Daimler-Benz's operations in Alabama and BMW's in South Carolina.

German industry has been treating the US as a Third World country for several years. Wages are low here, benefits are poor and the states compete against each other to bribe foreign companies to relocate. German unions have been trying to join with American ones to work on this problem, which hurts them both.

I suspect that the collapse of the Soviet empire has a lot to do with this. As was predictable, its main significance has been to return most of Eastern Europe to what it had been for five hundred years before—the original Third World. Areas that were part of the West—like the Czech Republic and western Poland—will end up resembling Western Europe, but most of Eastern Europe was submerged in deep Third World poverty, and they're going back to a kind of service role.

A while back, the *Financial Times* [of London] ran an article under the headline "Green Shoots in Communism's Ruins." The green shoots were

Western European industrialists' ability to pay Eastern European laborers much less than they pay "pampered western workers" with their "luxurious lifestyles" (as *Business Week* put it in another article).

Now they can get workers who are well-educated, because Communism did do a good job with that—even white and blue-eyed, though no one says that openly. They're also pretty healthy—maybe not for long, because the health systems are declining—but for a while, at least. And there's reasonable infrastructure.

Western companies typically insist on plenty of state protection, so when General Motors or VW invests in an auto plant in Poland or the Czech Republic, they insist on substantial market share, subsidies, protection, etc.—just as they do when they move into a Third World country or the US.

George Soros, the billionaire financier, has written several articles expressing his view that the spread of brutal global capitalism has replaced communism as the main threat to democratic societies.

It's not a new point. Working people 150 years ago were struggling against the rise of a system they saw as a great threat to their freedom, their rights and their culture. They were, of course, correct, and Soros is correct insofar as he reiterates that view.

On the other hand, he also makes the common assumption that the market system is spreading, which just isn't true. What's spreading is a kind of corporate mercantilism that's supported by—and crucially relies on—large-scale state power. Soros made his money by financial speculations that become possible when telecommunications innovations and the government's destruction of the Bretton Woods system (which regulated currencies and capital flow) allowed for very rapid transfers of capital. That isn't global capitalism.

As we sit here, the World Economic Forum is being held in Davos, Switzerland. It's a six-day meeting of political and corporate elites, with people like Bill Gates, John Welch of GE, Benjamin Netanyahu, Newt Gingrich and so on.

The companies represented at this forum do something like $4.5 trillion worth of business a year. Do you think it's a significant event that we should pay attention to?

Sure, we should pay attention to it, but I frankly wouldn't expect anything to come out of it that's not pretty obvious. Whether or not there's anything serious being discussed there, what reaches us will be mostly vacuous rhetoric.

We should also pay attention to the Trilateral Commission, but when you read its reports, they're rather predictable. The only really interesting thing I've ever seen from them was their first book—not because they were saying anything new, but because they were saying it so openly.

It's unusual to see an almost hysterical fear of democracy and a call for repressive measures to combat it expressed so explicitly. I suspect that's why the book was taken off the market as soon as it got to be noticed. I don't think it was meant to be read beyond select circles.

The Trilateral Commission, the Council on Foreign Relations and the like reflect a kind of consensus among business power, government power and intellectuals who aren't too far out of line. (They try to bring in other elements too; for instance, John Sweeney, president of the AFL-CIO, was at the Davos conference. They'd very much like to co-opt labor leadership, as they've done in the past.) There's plenty of evidence about what their views and goals are, and *why* they're their views and goals.

So you don't see any dark conspiracies at work in these organizations.

Having a forum in Switzerland would certainly be a pretty dumb way to plan a conspiracy.

I don't deny that there sometimes are conspiracies, by the way. In 1956, Britain, France and Israel planned an invasion of Egypt in secret. You can call that a conspiracy if you like, but it was really just a strategic alliance among huge power centers.

Admiral William Owens [former vice chair of the Joint Chiefs of Staff] and Joseph Nye [former Clinton Defense Department official who's now dean of the Kennedy School at Harvard] predict that the 21st century will be "the US century" because the US dominates world media, the Internet and telecommunications.

They also say that the US has an unrecognized "force multiplier" in its international diplomacy and actions, which comes from worldwide recognition of American democracy and free markets. They cite telecommunications and information technology, both textbook examples of how the public has been deluded into subsidizing private power.

The public assumes the risks and the costs, and is told it's defending itself against foreign enemies. *That's* supposed to be an illustration of democracy and markets. The delusion is so ingrained that nobody even comments on it.

Through Hollywood films and videos, TV and satellites, American culture is coming to dominate global culture.

When India began opening up its economy and American corporations were able to really start moving in, the first domain they took over was advertising. Very quickly, Indian advertising agencies became subsidiaries of big foreign ones, mostly based in the US.

The public relations industry has always aimed "to regiment the public mind every bit as much as an army regiments the bodies of its soldiers"—in the case of India, to create a system of expectations and preferences that will lead them to prefer foreign commodities to domestic ones.

There's been some resistance to this in India—massive demonstrations around Kentucky Fried Chicken, for example.

That's true in many places, even within Europe. There are moves towards creating a common European popular culture, common media and so on, making society more homogenous and controlled, but there are also moves in exactly the opposite direction—towards regionalization and the reviving of individual cultures and languages. These two movements are going on side by side, all over the world.

The US has created a global culture, but it's also created resistance to it. It's no more an inevitable process than any of the others.

In the last couple of years you've visited Australia, India, South America. What have you learned from your travels?

It's not hard to find out what's going on just sitting here in Boston.

But then you're just dealing with words on paper.

You're right—the colors become a lot more vivid when you actually see it. It's one thing to read the figures about poverty in India and another thing to actually see the slums in Bombay and see people living in hideous, indescribable poverty...and these are people who *have* jobs—they're manufacturing fancy leather clothes that sell on Madison Avenue and in shops in London and Paris.

It's a similar story throughout the world. But if you walk through downtown Boston, you'll also see appalling poverty. I've seen things in New York that are as horrifying as anything I've seen in the Third World.

Comparable to the *favelas* [shantytown slums] in Brazil?

It's hard to say "comparable." The poverty and suffering in Haiti or Rio de Janeiro or Bombay is well beyond what we have here—although we're moving in that direction. (As you know, black males in Harlem have roughly the same mortality rate as men in Bangladesh.)

But psychological effects are also crucially significant—how bad conditions seem depends on what else is around. If you're much poorer than other people in your society, that harms your health in detectable ways, even by gross measures like life expectancy.

So I'd say that there are parts of New York or Boston that are similar to what you find in the Third World. A Stone Age person could be very happy without a computer or a TV, and no doubt the people in the *favelas* live better than Stone Age people by a lot of measures—although they probably aren't as well-nourished or healthy.

But going back to your earlier point, seeing things firsthand gives them a vividness and significance you don't get by reading, and you also discover a lot of things that are never written about—like the way popular struggles are dealing with problems.

How can we organize against globalization and the growing power of transnational corporations?

It depends what time range you're thinking of. You read constantly that globalization is somehow inevitable. In the *New York Times,* Thomas Friedman mocks people who say there are ways to stop it.

According to him, it's not hawks and doves any more—there's a new dichotomy in the ideological system, between *integrationists,* who want to accelerate globalization, and *anti-integrationists,* who want to slow it down or modulate it. Within each group, there are those who believe in a safety net and those who believe people should be out on their own. That creates four categories.

He uses the Zapatistas as an example of the anti-integrationist pro-safety-net position, and Ross Perot as an example of the anti-integrationist anti-safety-net position, and dismisses them both as crazy. That leaves the two "sensible" positions, which are illustrated by Clinton (integrationist pro-safety-net) and Gingrich (integrationist anti-safety-net).

To test Friedman's analysis, let's look at Gingrich. To see if he represents maximization of free markets and undermining of safety nets, let's ask if he opposed the Reagan administration when it carried out the most protectionist policies since the 1930s? Did he object when Lockheed, his favorite cash cow, got big public subsidies for its merger with Martin Marietta? Did he resist the closing off of American markets to Japan, so our automotive, steel and semiconductor industries could reconstruct?

As these questions make clear, Gingrich is not an integrationist. He simply wants globalization when it's good for the people he's paid to represent, and not when it isn't.

What about safety nets? If he's opposed to welfare dependency, then he should certainly be opposed to providing federal subsidies to his constituents. But, in fact, he's a champion at bringing them home to his district.

So it's easy to see that Friedman's picture is mostly mythology. The fact that he can get away with it is the only interesting part of the story. The same is true of his belief that globalization is like a law of nature.

For one thing, in terms of gross measures like trade and investment flow (relative to the economy), globalization is more or less just getting back to where it was early in the century. (This is well-known, and has been pointed out in quite mainstream circles.)

There are also new factors. Capital flows are extremely fast and huge in scale. That's the result of two things: the telecommunications revolution (which is largely just another gift of publicly developed technology to private businesses), and the decision, during the Nixon administration, to break down the Bretton Woods system. But there's nothing *inevitable* about either—especially not the particular forms they've taken.

Also remember that huge corporations depend very extensively on their own states. Every single one of the companies on the *Fortune* 100 list of the largest transnational corporations has benefited from interventionist industrial policies on the part of the countries in which they're based, and more than 20 wouldn't have even survived if it weren't for public bailouts.

About two thirds of the international financial transactions take place within and between Europe, the US and Japan. In each of those places, parliamentary institutions are more or less functioning, and in none of them is there any danger of a military coup. That means it's possible to control, modify and even eliminate the supposedly uncontrollable forces driving us toward a globalized economy, even without substantial institutional change.

THE MYTH OF THIRD-WORLD DEBT

All over the world, but especially in the US, many workers vote against their own interests—assuming they vote at all.

I'm not sure that's true. Neither major party here represents workers' interests, but suppose there were candidates who did, and that US workers trusted them and were confident they'd try to do exactly what the workers wanted. There still might be a good reason not to vote for them.

When poor people in Central America vote for their own interests, the result is terror organized and directed by the superpower of the hemisphere, and supervised on the local level by the upper classes of that country. Many countries are so weak that they can't really solve their internal problems in the face of US power; they can't even control their own wealthy. Their rich have virtually no social obligations—they don't pay taxes and don't keep their money in the country.

Unless these problems are dealt with, poor people will sometimes choose to vote for oppressors, rather than suffer the violence of the rich (which can take the form of terror and torture, or can simply be a matter of sending the country's capital somewhere else).

Is capital flight a serious problem?

Not so much in the US, though even here the threat is able to constrain government planning (Clinton in 1993 is a well-known case). But look at virtually any country south of the Rio Grande. Take Brazil.

As happened almost everywhere in the Third World, Brazil's generals, their cronies and the super-rich borrowed huge amounts of money and sent much of it abroad. The need to pay off that debt is a stranglehold that prevents Brazil from doing anything to solve its problems; it's what limits social spending and equitable, sustainable development.

But if I borrow money and send it to a Swiss bank, and then can't pay my creditors, is that your problem or mine? The people in the slums didn't borrow the money, nor did the landless workers. In my view, it's no more the debt of 90% of the people of Brazil than it is the man in the moon's.

Discussions about a debt *moratorium* are not really the main point. If the wealthy of Brazil hadn't been out of control, Brazil wouldn't have the debt in the first place. Let the people who *borrowed* the money pay it back. It's nobody else's problem.

I discussed these matters all over Brazil—with poor people, at the national bishops' conference, with elite television reporters and high officials. They didn't consider it very surprising. In educated circles here, you could hardly get the basic issues taken seriously. One of the very striking differences you notice as soon as you get out of the First World is that minds are much less open here. We live in a highly indoctrinated society.

Breaking out of doctrinal shackles isn't easy. When you have as much wealth and power as we do, you can be blind and self-righteous; you don't have to think about anything. In the Third World, even wealthy and powerful people tend to have much more open minds.

Why hasn't foreign debt held back the developing countries of East Asia?

Japan, South Korea and Taiwan not only controlled labor and the poor, but also capital and the rich. Their debt went for internal investment, not export of capital.

Japan didn't allow export of capital until its economy had already reconstructed. South Korea didn't either, until forced to remove capital controls and regulation of private borrowing, largely under US pressure, in very recent years. (It's widely recognized that this forced liberalization was a significant factor in South Korea's 1997 liquidity crisis.)

Latin America has the worst income inequality in the world, and East Asia has perhaps the least. Latin America's typical imports are luxury goods for the wealthy; East Asia's have been mostly related to capital investment and technology transfer. Countries like Brazil and Argentina are potentially rich and powerful, but unless they can somehow gain control over their wealthy, they're always going to be in trouble.

Of course, you can't really talk about these countries as a whole. There are different groups within them, and for some of these groups, the current situation is great—just as there were people in India who thought the British Empire was fine. They were linked to it, enriched themselves through it, and loved it.

It's possible to live in the poorest countries and be in very privileged surroundings all the time. Go to, say, Egypt, take a limousine from the fancy airport to your five-star hotel by the Nile, go to the right restaurants, and you'll barely be aware that there are poor people in Cairo.

You might see some out the car windows when you're driving along, but you don't notice them particularly. It's the same in New York—you can somehow ignore the fact that there are homeless people sleeping in the streets and hungry children a couple of blocks away.

MEXICO, CUBA AND GUATEMALA

William Greider's book *One World, Ready or Not* describes the appalling economic conditions in Mexico. He says the country is very explosive, politically and socially.

That's absolutely correct. Throughout the 1980s, wages fell (it depends on how you measure them, but they were roughly cut in half, and they weren't high before that). Starvation increased, but so did the number of billionaires (mostly friends of the political leaders who picked up public assets for a few pennies on the dollar). Things finally collapsed in December 1994, and Mexico went into the worst recession of its history. Wages, already poor, declined radically.

A journalist I know at a Mexican daily called to interview me after the collapse. He reminded me of some interview of mine from a couple of months earlier where I'd said that the whole economy was going to fall apart.

I don't know much about Mexico or economics, but it was pretty obvious. Very short-term speculative funds were pouring in, and the speculative bubble had no basis. The economy was actually declining. Everybody could see this, including the economists at the international financial institutions, who (according to some specialists) kept it quiet because they didn't want to trigger the collapse.

Mexico was the star pupil. It did everything right, and religiously followed the World Bank and IMF's prescriptions. It was called another great economic miracle, and it probably was...for the rich. But for most of the Mexican people, it's been a complete disaster.

What do you hear from the Zapatistas?

Negotiations have been stalled for a couple of years, but I think it's clear what the government's strategy is: continue negotiations which won't get anywhere and ultimately, when the Zapatistas lose their capacity to arouse international interest, when people get tired of signing petitions—then the government will move in with force and wipe the Zapatistas out. That's my suspicion, anyway.

I think the only reason they didn't wipe them out right away is because the Zapatistas had so much popular support throughout Mexico and the world (which they managed to garner with a good deal of imagination). The fact that they've been able to remain in opposition for several years is pretty remarkable in itself.

But as it stands, it doesn't seem to me that they have any sort of a winning strategy. I don't say that as a criticism—I can't think of one either. Unless international support becomes really significant, I don't see how their position can be maintained.

What's happening with Cuba? A lot of people were bewildered when David Rockefeller [grandson of John D. and former chairman of the Chase Manhattan Bank] gave a party for Fidel Castro in New York in October 1995.

Cuba itself isn't of tremendous importance to the American economy. If it didn't exist, the effect wouldn't be noticeable. But the idea that other competitors are making inroads in this traditionally American market doesn't appeal to David Rockefeller and his friends. If investors elsewhere are going to break the American embargo, business here is going to call for it to end.

The same thing happened with Vietnam. US business was perfectly happy to punish Vietnam for failing to totally capitulate to US power. They would have kept their stranglehold on forever, dreaming up one fraudulent reason after another, except that by the mid-1980s Japan and other countries were starting to disregard the US embargo and move into the area, which has an educated population and low labor costs.

You followed the Jennifer Harbury case in Guatemala.

I wrote the introduction to her book, *Bridge of Courage*. She's a very courageous woman, and is still fighting. Sister Dianna Ortiz is another. It takes a lot of guts to do what these women have done.

Does the Guatemala peace treaty of December 1996 signal the end to this three-decade-old bloodbath?

I'm glad it's being signed, because it's a step forward. But it's also the very ugly outcome of one of the biggest state terror operations of this century, which started in 1954 when the US took part in overthrowing the only democratic government Guatemala ever had.

Let's hope the treaties may put an end to the real horrors. State terror has successfully intimidated people, devastated serious opposition, and made a government of right-wing business interests not only seem acceptable to many people, but even desirable.

BRAZIL, ARGENTINA AND CHILE

What kind of contact did you have with the media in Brazil, Argentina and Chile?

I immediately had a lot of contact with the mass media. That happens almost everywhere except in the US.

State television and radio?

Commercial stations too. The mass media are a lot more open there.

What about independent media?

There's an independent left journal published in São Paulo. It's in Portuguese, so I have only a superficial sense of what's in it, but the material looks extremely interesting. The journal is very well-designed and well-printed, as professional as *Harper's* or the *Atlantic*. We don't have anything like it here.

There are also more popular efforts. My wife and I spent an evening in one of the biggest of Rio's suburbs, Nova Iguaçu, where several million people— a mixture of poor, working-class, unemployed and landless peasants—live. (Unlike here, the rich live in the center of most Latin American cities, and the poor in the suburbs.) We were warned that we shouldn't go to Nova Iguaçu—too dangerous—but the people there were perfectly friendly.

We went with people from an NGO [nongovernmental (nonprofit) organization]—progressive artists, professionals and intellectuals who want to provide the population with an alternative to having their minds destroyed by commercial television. Their idea was to drive a truck with a huge screen into some public area and show documentaries dealing with real problems.

They spent a fair amount of time with the leaders of popular organizations in the community, figuring out how to make their points accessible, and how to put some humor in. I haven't seen the films, but apparently they were very well-done. But when they showed them in the poor neighborhoods, they completely bombed. People came by to check them out, watched for a while and left.

When the NGO did wrap-up sessions to try to figure out what happened, they discovered something very interesting: the leaders in the community spoke a different dialect, full of intellectual words and Marxist rhetoric, than the people they lived among. The process that made them leaders had also drawn them out of the mainstream of the community.

So the NGO went back, and this time they avoided the community leaders and tried to get members of the community—sixteen-year-old kids and the like—interested in writing the scripts and making the films. It wasn't easy, but it worked.

By the time we visited, which was a couple of years later, the NGO simply brought in the truck and the big screen. The people in the community—mostly young, but not entirely—wrote, shot and acted in the films themselves. They got a little technical assistance from the urban professionals, but essentially nothing else.

There was a big screen in the middle of a public area with little bars around. Lots and lots of people from the community were there—children and old people, racially mixed. It was in prime television time, nine o'clock in the evening. The people watching were obviously very much engaged in what was happening.

The dialog was in Portuguese, so I couldn't understand a lot of it, but I got enough to see that they were dealing with quite serious issues—although with humor and clowns mixed in. There was a skit on racism. (In theory, there isn't supposed to be any in Brazil.)

A black person would go to an office and ask for a job, then a white person would do the same, and of course they were treated totally differently. Everybody in the audience was laughing and making comments. There was a segment on AIDS, and something about the debt.

Right after the films ended, one of the actresses—who was quite good and looked about seventeen (at most)—started walking around the audience with a microphone, interviewing people about what they'd just seen. Their comments and criticisms were filmed live, eliciting more reactions.

This is very impressive community-based media of a sort that I've never seen before. It was in an extremely poor area, accomplished in spite of the initial failure I described. It was an experience I'm sure I would never have read about in a book.

We saw something similar in Buenos Aires. Some friends from the university took my wife and me to a shantytown where they work as activists. It's a very poor community in a very rich city; most of its inhabitants are Guaraní, indigenous people who migrated there from Paraguay.

School facilities there are awful, and any kid who causes even a small problem is just kicked out. An enormous number of the kids never make it through school. So some mothers set up what they call a cultural center, where they try to teach these kids reading and arithmetic, basic skills and little artwork, and also try to protect them from drug gangs. (It's very typical in such communities for women to do most of the organizing.)

Somehow they managed to find a small, abandoned concrete building and put a roof on it. It's kind of pathetic—about the size of this office. The provisions are so meager that even a pencil is a significant gift.

They also put out a journal. Written by the people in the shantytown, including some teenagers, it's full of information relevant to the community—what's going on, what the problems are.

Several of the women are becoming educated; a few are close to college degrees in professions like nursing. But they all say they'll never get out of the shantytown, no matter how many degrees they have. They haven't got a chance when they go for a job interview because they don't have the right clothes, the right look.

They're dedicated and they work hard, trying to save the children. They get some assistance from outside people, like those university friends of ours. The church also helps some. (This varies from community to community, depending on who the local priests are.)

They don't get any help from the government, I assume?

The Argentine government is in the grips of a neoliberal frenzy, obeying the orders of international financial institutions like the World Bank and the IMF. (*Neoliberalism* is basically nothing more than the traditional imperial formula: free markets for you, plenty of protection for me. The rich themselves would never accept these policies, but they're happy to impose them on the poor.)

So Argentina is "minimizing the state"—cutting down public expenditures, the way our government is doing, but much more extremely. Of course, when you minimize the state, you maximize something else—and it isn't popular control. What gets maximized is private power, domestic and foreign.

I met with a very lively anarchist movement in Buenos Aires, and with other anarchist groups as far away as northeast Brazil, where nobody even knew they existed. We had a lot of discussions about these matters. They recognize that they have to try to use the state—even though they regard it as totally illegitimate.

The reason is perfectly obvious: When you eliminate the one institutional structure in which people can participate to some extent—namely the government—you're simply handing over power to unaccountable private tyrannies that are much worse. So you have to make use of the state, all the time recognizing that you ultimately want to eliminate it.

Some of the rural workers in Brazil have an interesting slogan. They say their immediate task is "expanding the floor of the cage." They understand that they're trapped inside a cage, but realize that protecting it when it's under attack from even worse predators on the outside, and extending the limits of what the cage will allow, are both essential preliminaries to dismantling it. If they attack the cage directly when they're so vulnerable, they'll get murdered.

That's something anyone ought to be able to understand who can keep two ideas in their head at once, but some people here in the US tend to be so rigid and doctrinaire that they don't understand the point. But unless the left here is willing to tolerate that level of complexity, we're not going to be of any use to people who are suffering and need our help—or, for that matter, to ourselves.

In Brazil and Argentina, you can discuss these issues even with people in the highest political echelons, and with elite journalists and intellectuals. They may not agree with you, but at least they understand what you're talking about.

There are now organizations of landless peasants in Brazil.

Brazil has an enormous agrarian problem. Land ownership is highly concentrated, incredibly unequal, and an enormous amount of land is unused, typically because it's being held as a hedge against inflation or for investment purposes.

A very big and important organization, the Landless Workers' Movement, has taken over a lot of land. It has close links to the people in the *favelas,* who were mostly driven off their land too.

Brazil's army is very brutal, even more so since the coup of 1964. There's lots of killing and violence, one striking example being the murder of a couple of dozen peasants who took over some land in one of the northern regions. When I was in Brazil, informal judicial proceedings were being held about these murders, because the formal judicial system hadn't done anything about them.

You met with people in the Workers' Party.

It was very interesting. Brazil's Workers' Party is the largest labor-based party in the world. It has its problems, but it's an impressive organization with a radical democratic and socialist thrust, a lot of popular support and lots of potential. It's doing many important and exciting things.

Lula [Luis Inácio Lula da Silva, 1944– , founder and leader of the Workers' Party] is extremely impressive. If Brazil's presidential elections were even remotely fair, he would have won them. (It's not so much that votes were stolen but that the media resources were so overwhelmingly on the other side that there wasn't a serious election.)

Many workers have also become organized into rural unions, which are very rarely discussed. There's some degree of cooperation between the landless workers and groups in the *favelas*. Both are linked in some fashion to the Workers' Party, but the people I asked couldn't say exactly how. Everyone agrees that most of the landless workers support the Workers' Party, and vote for it, but organizationally they're separate.

What were your impressions of Chile?

I wasn't there long enough to get much of an impression, but it's very clearly a country under military rule. We call it a democracy, but the military sets very narrow bounds on what can happen. You can see it in people's attitudes—they know there are limits they can't go beyond, and in private they tell you that, with many personal examples.

THE MIDEAST

About 1980, you, Eqbal Ahmad [Pakistani scholar and activist, and professor at Hampshire College] and Edward Said [noted author, Palestinian activist and professor at Columbia] had a meeting with some top PLO officials. You've said you found this meeting rather revealing.

Revealing, but not surprising. It confirmed some very critical comments I'd made about the PLO in left journals a few years earlier, and which there was a big dispute over. The meeting was an attempt to make the PLO leadership, which happened to be visiting New York, aware of the views of a number of people who were very sympathetic to the Palestinians but quite critical of the PLO.

The PLO leadership wasn't interested. It's the only Third World movement I've ever had anything to do with that made no effort to build any kind of solidarity movement here, or to gain sympathy in the US for its goals.

It was extremely hard to get anything critical of Israel published, let alone distributed. The PLO could easily have helped, simply by buying books and sending them to libraries, but they were completely unwilling to do anything. They had huge amounts of money—they were brokering big deals between Kuwait and Hungary and who knows who else—but it was a very corrupt organization.

They insisted on portraying themselves as flaming revolutionaries, waving guns...which of course is going to alienate everyone. If they'd portrayed themselves as what they actually were—conservative nationalists who wanted to make money and maybe elect their own mayors—it would have increased the support in the United States for a Palestinian state from about 2 to 1 to about 20 to 1.

I think they believed that politics isn't about what the general population thinks or does, but about deals you make in back rooms with powerful people. (Incidentally, I heard much harsher criticisms of the PLO from activists and leaders in the Occupied Territories when I was there a few years later.)

If, as you've said, Israel is the local cop on the beat in the Mideast, why did the US go to such lengths to keep it out of the Gulf War?

Because if Israel had become directly involved, it would have been impossible for the US to keep the passive support of the major oil-producing countries in the region, and that's all Washington was really concerned with. Certainly they didn't need Israel's support to fight a war against a virtually defenseless Third World country. After the war, the US reestablished its domination of the region very strongly and told everybody, "What we say, goes" (as George Bush put it).

Eqbal Ahmad is rather pessimistic about Israel's long-term future. He says that sooner or later the relative weakness of Arab states will change.

I don't think it makes a lot of sense to try to make predictions about the long-term future. You can imagine a future in which the US is an embattled island, barely able to hold its own against the emerging powers of Asia that surround it. But as far as I can see, the US has about as much control and domination of the Middle East as any outside force could hope to maintain.

Our outpost there, Israel, is by far the main military, technological, industrial and even financial center. The huge oil resources of the region (which are still going to be needed for another couple of generations) are mostly in the hands of family dictatorships, brutal tyrannies that are highly dependent on the US and subordinated to its interests.

It's quite possible that the system will break down in the long term—but if you're talking about, say, two centuries from now, the US isn't even going to care about Mideast oil by then. For the kind of time frame within which policy planning makes any sense—which isn't long— things are working out as well as US planners could possibly have imagined. If it turns out, at some far distant time, that Israel is no longer necessary for US purposes, our support for Israel will end.

You've held that view for a very long time. You don't see any reason to change it.

None at all; in fact, I think we've had more and more evidence of it. For example, when a tiny disagreement came up between Israel and the US about how openly settlement of the West Bank should be pursued, President Bush didn't hesitate to make thinly veiled anti-Semitic remarks in front of a public audience. The Israeli lobby backed off and the US did what it wanted.

This is from Edward Said: "The crisis in Palestinian ranks deepens almost daily. Security talks between Israel and the PLO are advertised as a 'breakthrough' one day, stalled and deadlocked the next. Deadlines agreed upon come and go with no other timetable proposed, while Israel increases...the building of settlement residences (and) the punitive measures keeping Palestinians from leaving the territories and entering Jerusalem." He wrote this years ago, but it reads like today's news.

It does. The "peace process" goes up and down because the US-Israeli principles that define it have never offered anything meaningful to the Palestinians. The basic structure of US and Israeli policy has been clear for a long time. The principles are, strictly speaking, "rejectionist"—that is, they reject the rights of one of the two contestants in the former Palestine.

In the US, the term "rejectionist" is used in a racist sense, applying only to those who reject the rights of Jews. If we can bring ourselves to adopt nonracist usage, we will describe the US as the leader of the rejectionist camp.

In December 1989, when the Bush-Baker administration was supposed to be very hostile to Israel, the State Department came out with the Baker plan. It called for a "dialogue" in which only Palestinians acceptable to Israel and the US could participate. Discussion would be limited to implementation of Israel's official Shamir-Peres plan, which stipulated that:

- there can be no "additional Palestinian state" (other than Jordan, they meant)

- Israel should have effective control of as much of the Occupied Territories as it wants (however much that turns out to be)

- it's possible to hold "free elections" in territories that are under Israeli military supervision and with most of the educated elite in prison.

That was official US policy, under an administration that was supposed to be anti-Israel. (It was never accurately reported here. I wrote about it at the time.) The US was finally able to achieve these goals after the Gulf War, when the rest of the world backed off.

Large sections of the West Bank and Gaza are still occupied by the Israeli army.

The Oslo II Interim Agreement of September 1995 left Israel in control of about 70% of the West Bank, and in effective control of about another 26%. It put the urban centers of Palestinian towns in the hands of the Palestinian Authority, which is subordinate to Israel. (It's as if the New York police didn't have to patrol the worst slums—the local authorities did that for them—while the people in power took everything they wanted.)

I think Israel has way too much territory for its own potential needs or interests, and thus will probably be willing to relinquish some. If Israel is smart, it will work towards something like the Allon plan of 1968, which gave it control of the resources, water and usable territory (about 40% of the West Bank, the Gaza Strip and other areas), while relinquishing responsibility for the population.

Since then, the Gaza Strip has been more of a burden than something you'd want to hang onto. I think Israel will keep the so-called Gush Katif, down in the south; along with other parts they control, that probably amounts to 30% of all Gaza. (This is all for a couple of thousand Jewish settlers who use most of the resources, particularly water.) Israel will probably build strings of tourist hotels and keep up agricultural exports.

They'd be out of their minds to want to control Gaza City. They'd much rather leave it to the Palestinian Authority, along with the other urban centers and maybe 100 or so dots scattered around the West Bank and Gaza, with impassable roads connecting them.

There's a big superhighway system, but that's for the use of Israeli settlers and visitors. You can travel through the West Bank on these superhighways and barely know that Palestinians exist; you might see a remote village somewhere and maybe somebody selling something on the roadside.

It's like the Bantustans in South Africa, except that—as Norman Finkelstein has pointed out—the South African government gave much more support to the Bantustans than Israel is giving to those scattered regions.

In the epilogue to the latest edition of your book *World Orders, Old and New,* you say that Israel will eventually give some kind of state status to the Palestinians.

Israel and the US would be really stupid if they don't call whatever they decide to leave to Palestinian jurisdiction a state, just as South Africa insisted on calling the Bantustans "states," even though virtually no other country would do so. This new Palestinian "state" will get international recognition, however, because the US makes the rules.

What about the issue of Hebron and the agreement of January 1997?

It left the settlers in place, which is exactly what everyone should have expected them to do. There's no way for Israel to maintain control of the overwhelmingly Arab areas; they'd much rather have Palestinian police and joint Israeli-Palestinian patrols do that.

In the Israeli press, Clinton has been called "the last Zionist."

That was several years ago, in response to positions he took that were more extreme than almost anyone in mainstream Israeli politics.

Netanyahu got a five-minute ovation when he told the US Congress that Jerusalem will be the eternal, united capital of Israel, prompting him to remark, "If only I could get the Knesset [Israel's parliament] to vote like this."

Since 1967, US opinion—including liberal opinion—has pretty much been aligned with the more extremist elements in Israel. For example, the takeover of Arab East Jerusalem has been really ugly (I give a lot of details in *World Orders,* and elsewhere). What's now called Jerusalem is an area much bigger than anything that has ever been called Jerusalem in the past; in fact, it's a substantial part of the whole West Bank.

World opinion has repeatedly condemned this annexation as illegal. The US publicly agreed with this position, but meanwhile gave Israel authorization to do what it liked.

Much of the land annexation and Israeli settlements in Arab East Jerusalem is funded by money from the US.

Some of it's from American citizens, who probably are doing it tax-free (at least in part), which means that the rest of us are paying for it. Part of it comes from the US government, which again means that US taxpayers are financing it.

Theoretically, the US reduces its loan guarantees so as to exclude any funds spent for settling the West Bank, but the amount that's restricted is way below what's actually spent. Israelis know this is a joke—it's all over the Israeli press.

Furthermore, funds from the Jewish National Fund and several other so-called charitable organizations in the US also support settlements in various ways (in part indirectly, by funding development programs in Israel for Jewish citizens only, so that government funds can be transferred to subsidize settlers and infrastructure). That's again at taxpayer expense (since contributions to these charities are tax-deductible). All together, it amounts to quite a lot of money.

Many of the most militant settlers in the West Bank and Gaza are from the US. Does the American Jewish community foster this kind of militancy?

The American Jewish community is split, but a large number of the right-wing Jewish terrorists and extremists in Israel come from America. The Israelis don't like it—they don't want terrorists in their own society.

It's gotten to the point where there were even proposals—not entirely in jest—to control immigration from the US. Even very mainstream Israelis were saying, *Look, they're just sending us the crazies they don't know how to take care of. We don't want them.*

But I don't think this is unique to the American Jewish community. For whatever reason, diaspora communities tend to be, by and large, more extremist, chauvinistic and fanatic than people in the home country. That's true of just about every US immigrant society I can think of.

Support for the Israeli-US position in the Middle East has been largely uniform among American intellectuals, except for yourself, Edward Said and a handful of others). What do you attribute that to?

Things shifted very dramatically in 1967. The love affair between American intellectuals and Israel grew out of Israel's smashing military victory over all the Arab world. That was at a time when the US wasn't succeeding in its effort to demolish and control Indochina. There were all sorts of jokes about how we should send Moshe Dayan over there to show us how to do it.

There was also a lot of internal turmoil here, which worried elite opinion, including liberal opinion, a lot. Israel showed how to deal with the lower orders—really kick them in the face— and that won them a lot of points among American intellectuals.

There was an op-ed in the *New York Times* by an Israeli journalist, Ari Shavit, who also happens to be a veteran of Israel's 1978 invasion of Lebanon. In criticizing Israel's April 1996 attack on Lebanon, he wrote, "We killed [several hundred Lebanese] believing with absolute certitude that now, with the White House, the Senate and much of the American media in our hands, the lives of others do not count as much as our own." You had access to the Hebrew original of this. Did the *Times* make any changes?

There were a number of interesting changes. For example, Shavit didn't say "the American media"—he specified the *New York Times*. And he mentioned, as other institutions giving them confidence, AIPAC [the main pro-Israel lobbying group in the US], the [B'nai B'rith's] Anti-Defamation League, the Holocaust Museum [in Washington DC] and Yad Vashem [the Holocaust Memorial in Jerusalem].

This vulgar exploitation of the Holocaust is used to justify oppressive control over others. That's what Shavit was talking about—Israelis who think they can kill anybody, because they think that they have the *New York Times*, Yad Vashem and the Holocaust Museum behind them.

€AST TIMOR

José Ramos-Horta and Bishop Carlos Belo of East Timor, who both have labored against enormous odds, were honored with the 1996 Nobel Peace Prize. Any observations on that?

That was great—a wonderful thing. José Ramos-Horta has been a personal friend for twenty years. I haven't seen his official speech yet, but I ran into him in São Paulo and he was saying publicly that the prize should have been given to Xanana Gusmao, the leader of the resistance against Indonesian aggression, who's been in an Indonesian jail since 1992.

The recognition of the struggle is very important—or it will be, if we can turn it into something. The mainstream media will suppress it as quickly as possible; they'll give it some polite applause and then try to forget about it. If that happens, it will be our fault—nobody else's.

Right now, Clinton is planning to send arms to Indonesia. He'll get away with that unless there's a real public outcry. The Nobel Peace Prize offers a golden opportunity for people who care about the fate of a few hundred thousand people. But it's not going to happen by itself.

Some of the major issues have never even made it into the American press. For instance,

Timor's rich oil resources were part of the reason the US and Australia supported the Indonesian invasion in 1975. These resources are now being plundered under a disgraceful Australian-Indonesian treaty, with US oil companies involved. This issue has yet to be discussed, except really out at the fringes. We can do something about that.

Didn't you once go to the New York Times *editorial offices with someone from East Timor?*

At that time, they'd been refusing to interview Timorese refugees in Lisbon and Australia, claiming—like the rest of the mainstream media—that they had no access to them. I was asked to pay for plane tickets for some Timorese refugees in Lisbon to fly to New York. But the *Times* still wouldn't talk to them.

On another occasion, I managed to get the *Times* to interview a Portuguese priest, Father Leoneto do Rego, who had been living in the mountains with the Timorese resistance and had been driven out during the nearly genocidal campaign of 1978. That's when Carter increased the flow of weapons to Indonesia. The only reason they didn't murder Father Leoneto was because he was Portuguese.

He was a very interesting man and a very credible witness, a classmate of the cardinal of Boston, pretty hard to disregard—but nobody would talk to him. Finally I got the *Times* to interview him.

The article that resulted, by Kathleen Teltsch, was an utter disgrace. It said almost nothing about what was happening: there was one line that said something like, *Things aren't nice in Timor.* I suspect the badness of that article must have been what induced the *Times'* editors to run their first serious editorial on the issue.

Meanwhile, I was trying to get the *Boston Globe* to cover the story. They were just publishing State Department handouts and apologetics from Indonesian generals. They offered to let me write an op-ed, but I said, *No, I don't want to write an op-ed. I want one of your reporters to look into it.*

I finally got them to agree to look at the facts, but they didn't take them too seriously. Instead of putting an international reporter on the story, they gave it to a local reporter, Robert Levey. Fortunately, he was extremely good.

We helped him with some leads, and he picked up the ball and ran with it. Somebody in the State Department leaked him a transcript of the actual *New York Times* interview with Father Leoneto, which was very powerful and said extremely important things. His article was the best story on East Timor that had appeared in the American press.

All of this was in 1979 and early 1980. Before that, suppression of the East Timor issue had been total in the US press, and I mean *total;* when the atrocities peaked in 1978, there were literally *no* stories.

(It's not that nobody knew about East Timor. It was covered extensively back in 1974–75, when the Portuguese empire was collapsing— although the articles then were mostly apologetics and propaganda.)

The first article after the invasion that the *Reader's Guide to Periodical Literature* lists as specifically dealing with East Timor is one of my own; it was published in January 1979 in *Inquiry*, a right-wing libertarian journal I sometimes wrote for in those days. The article was based on testimony I'd given at the UN on the suppression of the issue by the Western—primarily the US—press. Arnold Kohen had discussed Timor in an earlier article about Indonesia he'd written in the *Nation*, and that was it for the journals.

Incidentally, here's a case where a very small number of people—the most important by far being Arnold Kohen—managed to save tens of thousands of lives, as a result of getting an issue into the public arena. The Red Cross was allowed in, and although the terror continued, it lessened.

It's also a case where the Internet made a difference. The East Timor Action Network was a very small and scattered group until Charlie Scheiner and others used the Internet to bring information to people who otherwise couldn't get it.

Friends in Australia had been sending me articles from the Australian press, but how many people have that luxury? Now everybody could get information very fast. The movement grew and became significant enough to have an impact.

INDIA

Didn't Adam Smith criticize the British crown for giving the East India Company a monopoly in India?

Yes, he did. He was very critical of what the British were doing there; he said the "savage injustice

100

of the Europeans" was destroying Bengal [in the northeast part of the country]. One example was the activities of the British East India Company [chartered in 1600 by Queen Elizabeth]. It forced farmers to destroy food crops and plant opium instead, which the Company then sold in China.

India had substantial industry in the 1700s, before the British crushed it. As late as the 1820s, the British were going to India to learn how to make steel. Bombay made locomotives that competed with those made in England.

India's steel industry might have developed—it just wasn't allowed to. Very heavy protectionism enabled England to develop while India was basically ruralized. There was virtually no growth in India under British rule.

India grew its own cotton, but Indian fabric was virtually barred from the British market because it undercut British textiles. The justification was, *Asian wages are so cheap we can't compete—we have to protect our markets.*

Adam Smith questioned that, and a recent dissertation in economic history at Harvard suggests he may have been right. According to this research, real wages may have been *higher* in India than in England, and Indian workers may also have had better benefits and more control over their work.

Fortunately for the US, things were different here. During the railroad boom of the 1800s, we were able to develop a steel industry because we imposed very high protectionist barriers to keep out British steel, which was better and cheaper.

We did the same thing in order to develop our textile industry fifty years before.

Adam Smith pointed out that British merchants and manufacturers used state power to make sure that their interests were "most peculiarly attended to," however grievous the impact on others— including not only people in the Third World, but also in England. The "principal architects of policy" got very rich, but the guys working in the satanic mills and in the British Navy surely did not.

Smith's analysis is truisms, but it's now considered extreme un-American radicalism, or something like that. The same pattern shows up today, when the US farms out export industries to El Salvador and Indonesia. A few people get richer and a lot of people don't—they may even get poorer—and our military power helps things stay that way.

In his book *Representations of the Intellectual,* Edward Said writes, "One of the shabbiest of all intellectual gambits is to pontificate about abuses in someone else's society and to excuse exactly the same practices in one's own." As examples, he cites de Tocqueville, who was critical of certain things in the US but cast a blind eye towards them in the French colony of Algeria, and John Stuart Mill, who had great ideas about democratic freedoms in England that he wasn't willing to apply to India.

Very far from it. Like his father, the famous liberal James Mill, John Stuart Mill was an official of the East India Company. In 1859, he wrote an absolutely appalling article about whether England should intervene in the ugly, dirty affairs of Europe.

A lot of people were saying, *It's none of our business. Let those backward people take care of themselves.* Mill objected, on the grounds that England had such a magnificent record of humane behavior that it would simply be unfair to the poor people of the world if England didn't intervene on their behalf. (You can see the same attitude in the US today, of course.)

The timing of Mill's article was interesting. It was written not long after the Indian Mutiny of 1857, which was suppressed with *extreme* brutality. The facts were well-known in England, but that didn't affect Mill's view of England as an angelic power that ought to help other countries out by intervening in their affairs.

You've just been to India for the first time in 25 years. What were the highlights of your visit?

I was there for just nine days, in six cities, so I don't have very deep impressions. It's a fascinating country, very diverse. Lots of resources, both human and material, are being wasted in a horrifying fashion.

There's extraordinary wealth and opulence, and incredible poverty (as there was under the British). The slums of Bombay are just appalling, and some rural areas are probably worse. India is still devastated by the effects of British colonialism, but many exciting things are going on as well.

India's constitution provides for village self-government, but that's apparently only been implemented in two states, West Bengal and Kerala [in southwestern India]. Both states are pretty poor, but because both have had Communist governments (West Bengal still does), and continue to have extensive social programs, neither foreign nor domestic investors seem to want to put money into them.

Despite that, Kerala is well ahead of other Indian states in health, welfare, literacy and women's rights. For instance, fertility rates have declined dramatically, and that's almost always a reflection of women's rights. I was there only briefly, but I could easily see the difference.

West Bengal is a much more complex area. Calcutta is a wreck—although not more so than other Indian cities, as far as I could see. (Based on what I'd read, I expected it to be worse than it seemed to be.)

The Bengali countryside is quite interesting. There's a history of peasant struggle in West Bengal, and it was apparently very violent in the 1970s. Indira Gandhi tried to put it down with a great deal of brute force, but it survived. They've gotten rid of most landlord control—maybe all of it.

I went to a part of West Bengal fifty miles or so from Calcutta. I was a guest of the government, accompanied by an Indian friend, an economist who works on rural development, and a government minister (who happened to have a PhD in economics from MIT). The villagers didn't know we were coming until about 24 hours before, so there was no particular preparation.

I've seen village development programs around the world, and this one was impressive. It's relatively egalitarian and appears to be really self-governing. We met with the village committee and a group of villagers, and they could answer every question we asked, which is unusual.

In other programs I've visited, people usually can't tell you what the budget is, what's planned for agricultural diversification next year, and so on. Here they knew all that stuff immediately, and spoke with confidence and understanding.

The composition of the committee was interesting. It was strikingly obvious that caste and tribal distinctions (tribal are usually worse) have been pretty much overcome. The governing committee was half women, one of them tribal. The guy who was more or less in charge of the committee was a peasant who had a little piece of land. Some of the people who spoke up were landless laborers who'd been given small plots.

They had an extensive land reform program and the literacy level has gone up. We went to a school that had a library of maybe thirty books, of which they were very proud.

Simple tube wells have been designed (with government support) that can be sunk by a group of families. Women, who've been trained to install and maintain them, seemed to be in charge. They took a tube well out for us and put it back in—also with lots of obvious pride.

We passed a place with a bunch of cans of milk out front, and I asked to stop in. It turned out to be a dairy cooperative set up by women. They said it wasn't particularly profitable, but they wanted to be self-employed and work together. These are all very important things, and unusual.

Unlike Kerala, Bengal was devastated by the British.

It was, but it was also very culturally advanced. For example, in the early 1800s, Bengal produced more books per capita than any place in the world. At that time, Dhaka [now the capital of Bangladesh] was so developed it was compared to London.

The Bengali literary tradition is extremely rich. Only the educated and rich took part in it (although even in the 19th century, caste differences were reported to be declining).

Kerala also has quite an interesting history. Although the British ruled it, they more or less left it alone. Apparently the local ruler initiated populist programs in order to gain popular support in a battle he was waging against feudal landlords.

The British were relaxed enough about Kerala to let these programs proceed, and after independence, they were picked up by the Communist government. By now, they're deeply imbedded, part of the way of life in Kerala, and when the Congress Party wins an election, it doesn't try to dismantle them.

One of the legacies of British colonialism is Kashmir [a province in the far north of India]. Did you have any discussions about that?

Most people I met said the Kashmiri separatists are terrorists. Some civil libertarians in India are pushing the issue courageously, and people do listen to them. But my impression (from six cities in nine days) is that it's not something a lot of Indians want to talk about honestly and openly.

Has the Indian government adopted neoliberal economics?

There's a tremendous amount of discussion, in the press and everywhere, about neoliberalism and structural adjustment. That's the main topic everybody wants to talk about.

They discuss it as if it's something new, but it's pretty much what India has been subjected to for three hundred years. When it's pointed out to them, they tend to recognize it, because they know their own history. That knowledge contributes to popular resistance to neoliberalism, which is why India hasn't accepted the harshest forms of it.

How far neoliberalism will get in India is an open question. For example, the government is trying to "liberalize" the media—which means, basically, sell them off to the likes of Rupert Murdoch. The media in India are mostly owned by the rich (as they are virtually everywhere), but they're resisting the attempt to turn them into subsidiaries of a half dozen international mega-corporations.

Although they're pretty right-wing, they'd rather run their own system of control internally than be taken over by outsiders. They've managed to maintain some sort of cultural autonomy...at least so far. There's some diversity in the Indian media—more than here—and that's very significant. It's much better to have your own right-wing media than Murdoch's.

As mentioned earlier, the same isn't true of India's small advertising industry—it's been mostly bought up by big, mostly American (maybe all American) multinationals. What they push—of course—is foreign products. That undermines domestic production and is harmful to the Indian economy, but many privileged people like it. Somebody always benefits from these programs.

Intellectual property rights are also a big issue. The new international patent rules are very strict and may well destroy the Indian pharmaceutical industry, which has kept drugs quite cheap. The Indian companies are likely to become subsidiaries of foreign firms, and prices will go up. (The Indian parliament actually voted the proposed patent rules down, but the government is apparently going to try to institute them anyway.)

There used to be only *process patents,* which permit people to figure out smarter ways to make products. The World Trade Organization has introduced *product patents;* they allow companies to patent not only a process, but also the product that's the result of the process. Product patents discourage innovation, are very inefficient and undermine markets, but that's irrelevant—they empower the rich and help big multinationals exercise control over the future of pharmaceuticals and biotechnology.

Countries like the US, England and Japan would never have tolerated anything remotely like product patents, or foreign control of their press, during their development. But they're now imposing this sort of "market discipline" on the Third World, as they did throughout the colonial period. That's one reason India is India, and not the US.

Another example is recruitment of scientists. Foreign firms pay salaries way beyond what Indian researchers are used to, and set up research institutes with facilities Indian scientists can't dream of getting anywhere else. As a result, foreign firms can skim off the best scientists.

The scientists may be happy, and the companies are happy. But it's not necessarily good for India, which once had some of the most advanced agricultural research in the world.

An Indian farmer used to have a place he could go to and say, *There's some funny pest in my fields. Can you take a look at it?* But now that's being bought up by foreign firms, and will therefore be oriented towards export crops for specialized markets, and subsidized foreign imports that will undercut domestic production.

There's nothing new about this. It's part of a long history of "experiments" carried out by the powerful of the world. The first major one in India was what the British called the Permanent Settlement of 1793, which rearranged all the land holdings in Bengal.

When the British Parliament looked into this thirty or forty years later, they conceded that it was a disaster for the Bengalis. But they also pointed out that it enriched the British, and created a landlord class in Bengal, subordinated to British interests, that could control the population.

We've already discussed a recent example of such experiments, in Mexico. Such experiments regularly seem to fail for the experimental animals, but succeed for the *designers* of the experiment. It's an oddly consistent pattern. If you can find an exception to that pattern over the last couple of hundred years, I'd be interested in hearing about it. I'd also be interested in knowing who in the mainstream talks about it, since I haven't been able to find anyone.

Getting free from the colonial powers generated a tremendous burst of energy in India, as did presenting a neutralist challenge to US domination.

That challenge is pretty much gone—from Indian policy, at least, if not from the general population.

The US was very much opposed to Indian independence and also, of course, to Nehru's attempts at nonalignment. Any Indian with a streak of independence was bitterly hated and condemned by US policymakers. Eisenhower called Nehru a "schizophrenic" who suffered from an "inferiority complex" and had a "terrible resentment" of "domination by whites" (really surprising, given how the British treated India).

The US basically brought the Cold War to South Asia by arming Pakistan, which was part of our system of control of the Middle East. It ended up in India and Pakistan fighting several wars with each other, sometimes with American arms.

US policymakers were also worried about Indonesia. In 1948, George Kennan, one of the chief architects of US policy, described Indonesia as "the most crucial issue of the moment in our struggle with the Kremlin." (The USSR wasn't really the issue, of course—that was just code for "independent Third World development.")

He was very much afraid that a Communist Indonesia would be an "infection" that "would sweep westward through all of South Asia"—not by conquest, of course, but by example. That concern wasn't really overcome until the mass slaughter in Indonesia in 1965, which the US government, the press and other commentators were all exhilarated about.

They had the same fear about China—not that it was going to conquer South Asia, but that it was developing in ways that might be a model for other Asian countries. US policymakers remained ambivalent toward India. They had to support it as an alternative model to China, but they hated to do it, because India was following a somewhat independent line and had established close relations with the Soviet Union.

The US gave some aid to India, which was supposed to be the democratic alternative to China. But it was given grudgingly, and the US wouldn't permit India to develop its own energy resources; instead, they had to import oil, which was much more expensive. India's petroleum resources are apparently significant, but they still haven't been developed.

The results of US ambivalence towards India have sometimes been pretty ugly. Right after independence, in the early 1950s, India had a very serious famine, in which millions of people died. US internal records show that we had a huge food surplus, but Truman refused to send any, because we didn't like Nehru's independence. When we finally did send some, it was under stringent conditions. (There's a good book on this by historian Dennis Merrill.)

What was your overall impression of India?

The questions being debated in India—whether to use import restrictions, or to adopt neoliberal policies—can't really be answered in general. Like debt, import restrictions aren't good or bad in themselves—it depends on what you use them for. In Japan, Taiwan and South Korea, where they were used to build up a domestic industrial base and market (as in Britain and the US in earlier years), they proved to be a good idea (for the home country, at least). But if you use them to protect an inefficient system and the super-rich who profit from it, they're bad.

Here's a personal anecdote that illustrates things that are very real, but that you can't measure. After a talk in Hyderabad, some friends were driving me to the airport. When we were about two miles away, the traffic completely froze up. Every inch of the road was covered by a bicycle, a rickshaw, an oxcart, a car or whatever. The people were sort of quiet; nobody was making a fuss.

After about twenty minutes, we realized that the only way to get to the airport on time was to walk. So my friends and I started threading our way through this immense traffic jam.

Finally we got to a big highway that was blocked off. There are lots of cops and security forces everywhere in India, but here there were *tons.* My friends talked them into letting us cross the road, which we weren't supposed to do, and we finally made it to the airport (which was semi-functional because it was cut off from the city).

Why was the highway closed down? There were signs next to it saying *VVIP*, which I was told means *Very Very Important Person*. Because some "VVIP"—we later found out it was the prime minister—was expected at some indefinite time in the future, the city was closed down.

That's bad enough—what's worse is the fact that people tolerated it. (Just imagine the same thing happening here in Boston, say.) Feudalistic attitudes run very deep in India, and they're going to be hard to uproot.

That's what was so striking about the village in West Bengal. Poor, landless workers, including lots of women, were active and engaged. You can't put numbers on that kind of change, but it makes a huge difference. That's real popular resistance and activism, like the democratic institutions that developed in Haiti before Aristide's election (and that still exist there) and what happened in Central America in the '70s and '80s.

(In Haiti, democracy elicited instant US hostility and a murderous military coup, tacitly supported by the US; in Central America, a US-run terrorist war. In both places, the US permitted democratic forms after establishing conditions that prevented them from functioning—amidst much self-congratulation about the nobility of our leaders.)

What has to be overcome in India is enormous. The inefficiency is unbelievable. While I was there, the Bank of India came out with an estimate that about a third of the economy is "black"—mainly rich people who don't pay their taxes. Economists there told me one-third is an underestimate. A country can't function that way.

As elsewhere, the real question for India is, can they control their own wealthy? If they can figure out a way to do that, there are lots of policies that might work.

INTERNATIONAL ORGANIZATIONS

In *World Orders, Old and New,* you say that the UN has become virtually an agency for US power.

The UN mostly does what the US—meaning US business—wants done. A lot of its peacekeeping operations are aimed at maintaining the level of "stability" corporations need in order to do business. It's dirty work and they're happy to have the UN do it.

If that's so, how do you explain the hostility toward [former UN Secretary General] Boutros Boutros-Ghali?

In the first place, there was an element of racism there—even though the next choice, Kofi Annan, was also from Africa. When George Bush talked about "Bou-Bou Ghali," nobody batted an eyelash, although I doubt very much that a presidential candidate in the US would survive very long if he referred to the former prime minister of Israel as, say, "Itzy-Schmitzy Rabin."

There's a lot of opposition to the UN on the extreme right. Some of it's tied in with fantasies about black helicopters and loss of sovereignty to world government. But some of it's simply a case of avoiding blame.

Take the atrocities carried out in Somalia, where the US quietly concedes that thousands of

Somali civilians—perhaps up to ten thousand—were killed by US forces. If somebody threatened US forces, they'd call in helicopter gunships. That doesn't sound so heroic, so the resulting catastrophes became the fault of the UN.

Similarly, the US evaded the burdens and difficulties of the conflict in the former Yugoslavia until things were more or less settled, then moved in and took over (effectively imposing a kind of partition between Greater Croatia and Greater Serbia). That way, the US could blame everything that went wrong on the UN. Very convenient.

It's easy to focus anti-UN hostility on the secretary general. Let's kick him in the pants, and kick the rest of the world in the pants too. Why should we bother with what other countries think about us anyway?

Do you think the very critical UN report on the Israeli attack on the UN compound in Qana, Lebanon may have been a factor in undermining support for Boutros-Ghali?

It might have been a small factor, but who paid any attention to it? It was so marginalized that I frankly doubt it had much effect. Amnesty International came out with a study that strongly corroborated the UN report. That also disappeared very quickly; I'm not even sure it was reported on at all.

These sorts of things can be brushed off very quickly when they're inconvenient for power and career interests. Both reports are quite shocking, and confirmed by veteran journalists on the scene (notably Robert Fisk). But it's the wrong story.

The basic reason there's hostility to international institutions here is that they don't always do exactly what the US orders them to do. The World Court is a perfect example. The US government isn't going to accept being condemned by it—as it was in 1986, for "unlawful use of force" against Nicaragua. The Court ordered the US to desist and pay substantial reparations, and ruled explicitly that no aid to the Contras could be considered "humanitarian." We don't have to waste time noting how the US, the press and educated opinion reacted to this.

The International Labor Organization is another example. Not only does it stand up for workers' rights, but it condemned the US for violating international labor standards. So it's dismissed, and the US refuses to pay the roughly $100 million owed to it.

The US has little use for the UN Development Program or the Food and Agriculture Organization, since they're mostly concerned with developing countries. UNCTAD (the UN Conference on Trade and Development) has, to some extent, advocated the interests of developing countries and has been an expert critical voice opposing certain Washington policies, so it's been undermined and tamed as well.

As soon as UNESCO called for opening up the world information system, it was out of luck. The US forced it to abandon its evil ways, and significantly modified its role.

The attack on these organizations is all part of reconstructing the world in the interests of the most powerful and the most wealthy. There's lots wrong with the UN, but it's still a somewhat democratic institution. Why tolerate that?

The US attitude was expressed rather neatly by Madeleine Albright in a remark which, as far as I know, wasn't reported. She was trying to get the Security Council to accept one of our punitive actions toward Iraq; none of the other countries wanted to go along with it, since they recognized that it was really just a part of US domestic politics. So she told them that the US will act "multilaterally when we can and unilaterally as we must." So would anyone else, if they had the power.

The US owes the UN over $1 billion—more than any other country.

Of course. Why should we spend money on anybody but the rich?

The World Trade Organization is the successor to GATT [the General Agreement on Tariffs and Trade, the international treaty that regulated world trade]. Has the US been fairly happy with the WTO?

Not entirely. The US has been brought up more than once for violation of WTO principles, and was also condemned by the GATT council earlier. But in general, the US is more or less favorable to the WTO, whose mixture of liberalization and protectionism is pretty much tailored to the needs of powerful transnational corporations and financial institutions.

The Uruguay Round treaty that led to the WTO was called a free trade agreement, but it's really more of an investor rights agreement. The US wants to use WTO rules in areas it expects to dominate, and is certainly in a position to cancel any rule it doesn't like.

For example, a while back the US forced Mexico to cut back exports of its tomatoes. It's a violation of NAFTA and WTO rules and will cost Mexican producers close to a billion dollars a year. The official reason was that Mexican producers were selling tomatoes at a cost American producers can't match.

If the WTO rules in favor of the European Union's request to condemn the Helms-Burton Act [which strengthened the US embargo against Cuba] as an illegal interference with world trade, the US will just go on acting unilaterally. If you're powerful enough, you can do whatever you want.

What do you think of the expansion of NATO?

I don't think there's a simple answer to that—it depends how the economic and political structure of Eastern Europe and Western Asia evolves.

As mentioned above, when the Cold War ended I expected that the former Soviet empire would pretty much revert to what it had been before. The areas that had been part of the industrial West—the Czech Republic, western Poland, Hungary—would essentially be reintegrated into the West, and the other parts, which had been Third World before the Soviet Union, would return to that status, with substantial poverty, corruption, crime and so on. Partial extension of the NATO system to industrial—or partially industrial—countries like the Czech

Republic, Poland and Hungary would help formalize all this.

But there will be conflicts. Europe and the US have differing expectations and goals for the region, and there are also differences within Europe. Russia isn't a trivial force either; it can't be disregarded and doesn't like being excluded. There are more complex power plays, like the jockeying that's going on around the oil fields in Central Asia, where the *people* involved won't have much of a voice in the process.

In the case of NATO, there are other factors, like the special interests of military industry, which is looking forward to a huge market with NATO expansion and standardization of weapons (which are mainly produced by the US). That translates into another substantial taxpayer subsidy to high-tech industry, with the usual inefficiencies of our system of industrial policy and "state socialism for the rich."

THE US LEFT
(AND IMITATIONS THEREOF)

ARE LEFT AND RIGHT MEANINGFUL TERMS?

Historically, the left has been somewhat ambivalent about political power. The right has no such inhibitions—they *want* political power.

I don't much like the terms *left* and *right*. What's called the left includes Leninism, which I consider ultra-right in many respects. The Leninists were certainly very interested in political power—in fact, more so than anyone.

Leninism has nothing to do with the values of the left—in fact, it's radically opposed to them. That was recognized at the time by mainstream left Marxists like Anton Pannekoek, Paul Mattick and Karl Korsch. Even Trotsky had predicted that the Leninists would turn to dictatorial rule (before he decided to join them).

[The Polish-German revolutionary] **Rosa Luxemburg** [1871–1919] warned of the same things (in a more or less friendly way, because she didn't want to harm the movement). So did Bertrand Russell. And, of course, most of the anarchists did.

Conventional terms of political discourse like *left* and *right* have been almost evacuated of meaning. They're so distorted and irrelevant it's almost better to throw them out.

Take Witness for Peace, which has been a very important organization since the 1980s. People from an imperial country actually went down and lived in Third World villages, in the hope that a white face might protect the inhabitants from state terrorists organized by their own country. That's never happened before.

Was that left or right? It certainly represents the traditional ideals of the left, like justice, freedom, solidarity, sympathy. On the other hand, a lot of it came out of the conservative Christian community. I don't know where to put Witness for Peace on any political spectrum. It's just human beings acting decently.

What's currently lambasted as "political correctness" is supposed to be left. But in many places I go—including campuses that are extremely conservative, where there is hardly any political activity—very delicate judgments are made about just what it's OK to say with regard to minuscule questions of gender, race, color, etc. Is that left or right? I don't know.

Part of what the propaganda system does is deprive terms of meaning. It probably starts at some relatively conscious level and then just gets into your bones. Sometimes it's done quite deliberately.

One dramatic case in recent years is the disappearance of the word *profits*. Profits don't exist anymore—just jobs. So when Clinton came back from Indonesia with a $40-billion contract for Exxon, the media all talked about jobs for Americans. But profits for Exxon? Perish the

NOAM CHOMSKY &. THE COMMON GOOD

thought. (Exxon's stock shot up, but that's just because investors were so delighted about the new jobs.)

That's conscious evacuation of meaning, and even the left falls into it, talking about how Congressmen vote for the Pentagon because they want jobs for their district. Are *jobs* what Congressmen are worried about, not profits and public subsidies for firms?

In a lead story, the *New York Times Week in Review* made an amazing discovery: the new kind of "populism"—as practiced by Steve Forbes, Pat Buchanan and the like—is different from the old kind of populism. The old kind opposes big corporations and plutocrats; the new kind *is* big corporations and plutocrats. That you can have a character like Steve Forbes on the national scene without people cracking up with laughter shows how intense the propaganda is.

THE NARCISSISM OF SMALL DIFFERENCES

In his book *The Twilight of Common Dreams,* Todd Gitlin says the left is polarized by identity politics, which he calls the "narcissism of small differences." He writes, "The right has been building...but the left has been...cultivating difference rather than commonality."

The left does tend to get caught up in sectarianism, but I think he's describing something that's happening in the country in general, not just in what might be called realistically "the left." The activism of the '60s had a very civilizing effect—it brought to the fore all sorts of oppression and discrimination that had been suppressed.

122

The killing off of the native populations—which had been pretty much ignored even in scholarship—was put on the agenda for the first time. Environmental issues (which basically have to do with the rights of future generations), respect for other cultures, the feminist movement—these had all existed in some form earlier, but they really took off in the '70s and spread throughout the whole country. The Central America solidarity movement wouldn't have existed in the form it did if not for what happened in the '60s.

Concerns about oppression, authority and rights can sometimes take the unhealthy forms that Gitlin is criticizing, but they needn't, and commonly didn't.

Louis Farrakhan and the Million Man March seemed to be the epitome of identity politics, since the participants were defined not only by race but by gender. What did you think of that?

I think it's a more complicated phenomenon. There were also elements of self-help, rebuilding viable communities and lives, taking responsibility for what you do. These are all good things.

But Farrakhan's economic program is small-scale capitalism.

I didn't see anything much in the way of an economic program, but when you're crushed, even small-scale capitalism can be a step forward. It shouldn't be the end of the road, obviously, but it can be a step.

I think this movement is much more nuanced than some of the commentary has assumed. It has opportunities to go a lot of different ways, and how it comes out depends on what people do with it.

There's a reason why it's men—look at what's happened to black men in the last twenty years. There's been a virtual war against minorities and the poor. It included plenty of scapegoating, like Reagan's anecdotes about black welfare mothers with Cadillacs, and the Willie Horton concoctions. The fraudulent war on drugs, which has little to do with drugs or crime, is another part of it.

Michael Tonry points out that those who crafted the programs had to know they were going right after young blacks. Every indicator pointed in that direction. Tonry further points out that, in the law, conscious foreknowledge is evidence of intent of criminal action.

I think he's right about that. The so-called "war on drugs" was in no small measure a criminal attempt to criminalize the black male population and, more generally, segments of the population that are sometimes called "disposable people" in our Latin American dependencies, because they don't contribute to profit-making.

You're aware of Farrakhan's comments on...

I don't have anything to say about Farrakhan— I'm talking about the phenomenon. Probably he's just an opportunist trying to get power—that's what leaders usually are. But I don't know what's in his mind, and I don't presume to judge what he's up to. I'm too far out of it.

Christopher Hitchens, who writes for the *Nation* and *Vanity Fair,* recalls that the first time he heard the slogan "the personal is political," he felt a deep sense of impending doom. To him, the slogan sounds escapist and narcissistic, implying that nothing will be required of you except being able to talk about yourself and your own oppression. He was talking about the growth of identity movements.

I agree with him. It certainly opened itself up to that, and it's been exploited that way, sometimes in ugly—and often in comical—ways. But it doesn't only have that aspect. It can also mean that people have the right to adopt their individual ways of living if they want, without oppression or discrimination.

POSTMODERNISM

A respected NYU physics professor, Allen Sokal, got an article published in *Social Text,* which has been described as the leading cultural studies journal in the country. To point out the decline in intellectual rigor in certain parts of American academia, he intentionally filled the article with errors. What do you make of that?

His article was cleverly done. He quoted—accurately—from advanced physics journals, then juxtaposed quotes from postmodern critiques of science, including *Social Text*, as if the former somehow supported the latter. No one with any familiarity with the material could read the article without laughter.

Sokal's point was that postmodern critiques of science are based on ignorance—they're flights of fancy that lack minimal critical standards. There's something healthy about this sort of criticism, but his article is also going to be used as a weapon against attitudes and work that have merit.

It was immediately interpreted by the *New York Times* and the *Wall Street Journal* as just one more demonstration that some sort of left-fascist political correctness movement has taken over academic life—when what's really going on is a significant right-wing assault against academic freedom and intellectual independence.

Well, we live in this world, unfortunately. What we do is going to be used by powerful people and institutions for their purposes, not for ours.

Postmodernists claim to represent some kind of a subversive critique. Have you been able to detect that?

Very little of it. I'm not a big expert on postmodern literature; I don't read it much, because I find most of it pretty unilluminating, often complicated truisms or worse. But within it there are certainly things that are worth saying and doing. It's very valuable to study the social, institutional and cultural assumptions within which scientific work is done, but the best work of that sort isn't by postmodernists (at least as far as I can understand their work).

For instance, fascinating work has been done in the last thirty or forty years on what Isaac Newton, the great hero of science, actually thought he was doing. His theory of gravity was very disturbing to him and to everyone else at the time. Because gravity works at a distance, Newton agreed with other leading scientists of his day that it was an "occult force," and spent most of the rest of his life trying to come to terms with that unacceptable conclusion.

In the final edition of his great work, the *Principia,* he said that the world consists of three things: active force, passive matter and some semi-spiritual force (which, for various reasons, he identified with electricity) that functions as an intermediary between the two. Newton was an expert on church history (physics was a very small part of his interests) and the framework for his theory of an intermediary force was the fourth-century Arian heresy, which said that Jesus is semi-divine, not divine, and acts as an intermediary between God and man.

After Newton's death, his papers were given over to the physicists at Cambridge University. They were appalled by what they found in them, so they simply gave them back to his family, which held onto them and never published them.

Around the 1930s, they started selling the material off; [the British economist John Maynard] Keynes was one of those who recognized their enormous value. After WWII, some of this stuff started surfacing at antique dealers, and scholars began to gather it together and do important analytical work.

Now that's serious cultural-sociological analysis of some of the greatest moments of science, and there's plenty more like it. You can bring it right up to the present. People do scientific work within a framework of thought, and their work is affected by cultural factors, by power systems, by all sorts of things. Nobody denies that.

What the postmodernists claim to be fighting is *foundationalism,* the idea that science is divorced from society and culture and provides foundations for certain, absolute truth. Nobody has believed that since the 1700s.

From what I've looked at, I find postmodernism very dense, jargon-laden and hard to read.

I do too. A lot of it has the appearance of a kind of careerism, an escape from engagement.

But they claim to be socially engaged.

In the '30s, left intellectuals were involved in worker education and writing books like *Mathematics for the Millions*. They considered it an ordinary, minimal responsibility of privileged people to help others who'd been deprived of formal education to enter into high culture.

Today's counterparts of these '30s left intellectuals are telling people, *You don't have to know anything. It's all junk, a power play, a white male conspiracy. Forget about rationality and science.* In other words, put those tools in the hands of your enemies. Let them monopolize everything that works and makes sense.

Plenty of very honorable left intellectuals think this tendency is liberatory, but I think they're wrong. A lot of personal correspondence on related topics between me and my close, valued old friend Marc Raskin has been published in a book of his. There are similar interchanges in *Z Papers* in 1992–93, both with Marc and a lot of other people with whom I basically feel in sympathy, but with whom I differ very sharply on this issue.

EXCOMMUNICATED BY THE ILLUMINATI

You've long been excommunicated, if I can use that word, not only from the mass media but also from the "illuminati" circles of the Upper West Side and their publications, like the *New York Review of Books* [usually referred to simply as the *New York Review*].

It has nothing to do with me.

What happened?

The *New York Review* started in 1964. From about 1967 to about 1971, as political engagement grew among young intellectuals, it was open to dissident analysis and commentary from people like Peter Dale Scott, Franz Schurmann, Paul Lauter, Florence Howe and myself.

Then, within a few years, we all disappeared from its pages. I think what happened is that the editors wanted to keep ahead of the game. They knew their audience and couldn't fail to see that the young intellectuals who constituted a large part of it were changing.

It ended for me personally in late January 1973. Nixon and Kissinger's "peace treaty" with Hanoi had just been announced. The *New York Times* published a big supplement that included the text of the treaty and a long interview with Kissinger in which he went through the treaty paragraph by paragraph. The war was over, he said, everything was just fantastic.

I was suspicious. Something similar had happened about three months earlier, in October 1972, when Radio Hanoi had announced a peace agreement the US had been keeping secret. It was the last week of Nixon's re-election campaign.

Kissinger went on television and said, *Peace is at hand.* Then he went through the peace agreement, rejected every single thing in it, and made it very clear that the US was going to continue bombing.

The press only picked up Kissinger's first line, *Peace is at hand.* Wonderful. It's all over. Vote for Nixon. What he was actually saying was, *We're not going to pay any attention to this, because we don't want this agreement, and we're going to keep bombing until we get something better.*

Then came the Christmas bombings, which didn't work. The US lost a lot of B-52s, and faced big protests all around the world. So they stopped the bombings and accepted the October proposals they'd previously rejected. (That's not what the press said, but that's essentially what happened.)

The January farce was the same. Kissinger and the White House made it clear and explicit that they were rejecting every basic principle of the treaty they were compelled to sign, so that they could go on with the war, seeking to gain what they could.

I was pretty angry. I happened to have a talk scheduled for a peace group at Columbia that evening. I called Robert Silvers, a friend who was the editor of the *New York Review,* and asked him if we could meet for dinner. We spent an hour or two going through the texts in the *Times'* special supplement. It was easy enough to see what they meant.

I said, *Look, I'd like to write about this. I think it's the most important thing I'll ever write, because you know as well as I do the press is going to lie flat out about it. The destruction and killing will go on, and then, when the whole thing collapses because of the US initiatives, they're going to blame the Vietnamese* (which is exactly what happened).

He said, *Don't worry—you don't need to write an article. I'll make sure your point of view gets in.* It was supposed to be in an article written by Frances FitzGerald, but it wasn't; she didn't understand or didn't agree with the point.

I published articles about this right away, but in *Ramparts* and in *Social Policy*. That was essentially the end of any association with the *New York Review*. We understood each other.

Why are you in the *Nation* so infrequently?

It's complicated. I don't recall any contact with them until about the late 1970s, I guess. At that point I wrote some book reviews for them. Occasionally they'd invite me to take part in a symposium, but mostly we were sort of at arm's length. We didn't really see things the same way.

In the late '80s, I interviewed Victor Navasky [then the *Nation*'s editor, now its publisher and editorial director]. He said he was uncomfortable with your views on the Middle East.

Victor, who I like, once called me to say that people kept asking him why I wasn't in the magazine. He explained to them that it was because I kept sending him huge articles that were way too long. In fact, the only article I'd ever submitted to the *Nation* was about two pages long.

It was right after the bombing of Beirut ended in mid-August of 1982. There was a flurry of talk about how there was going to be peace and everything was going to be wonderful.

My article, based mainly on the Israeli press, said this was nonsense, that the US and Israel intended to continue fighting, and that there were going to be further atrocities. (I didn't know then, of course, that the massacres at the Sabra and Shatila Palestinian refugee camps were going to take place a few weeks later, but that was the sort of thing I was anticipating.)

I sent the article to the *Nation* and never heard a word from them. It's the only one I've ever submitted. Actually, that's the reason I wrote my book *The Fateful Triangle.* I was so infuriated at my inability to get one word even into the left press about Sabra and Shatila that I figured I'd better write a book about it. (I wrote it mostly at night, because I had no other free time.)

Somebody asked me to ask you about critiques of your work, so let's talk about an article by Richard Wolin in *Dissent,* a very serious and scholarly journal. He wrote that your book *World Orders, Old and New* is a "heavy-handed, fact-filled, citation-laden jeremiad," that you're "ideologically obsessed," that your views coincide with those of the far right, and that you have a "long-standing contempt for Israel."

If that's the most cogent criticism you can find, there's nothing much to talk about. I wasn't going to respond to that article, but some friends associated with *Dissent* asked me to, so I did, putting aside the flow of insults and keeping to the few identifiable points.

Wolin's main complaint was that I'm always saying the US is a "totalitarian" and "fascist" country. It just so happened that articles appeared in London and Greece at about the same time I got that issue of *Dissent*. Both raised the question I'm commonly asked overseas: *Why do I keep talking about the US as the freest country in the world?* That's what people in other countries hear. What Wolin hears is my calling the US a totalitarian, fascist state.

He also says I use Orwellisms. That refers to my quoting a few sentences of an unpublished article of Orwell's that was supposed to be an introduction to *Animal Farm*. Orwell pointed out that in a very free society (he was talking about England), there are all sorts of ways to keep unpopular ideas from being expressed.

One factor is that the press is owned by wealthy men who have every reason not to have certain ideas expressed. He identified education as another factor. When you go through Oxford or Cambridge, you learn that there are certain things it "wouldn't do to say." If you don't learn that, you're not in the system.

What can you say about being criticized for having a fact-filled, citation-laden book? They've got you coming and going. If you don't cite facts…

It's not just me—any critic on the left is going to have to face that. If you don't footnote every word, you're not giving sources—you're lying. If you *do* footnote every word, you're a ridiculous pedant. There are lots of devices in relatively free societies to achieve the goals that Orwell described.

WHAT YOU CAN DO

SIGNS OF PROGRESS (AND NOT)

Over the last twenty or thirty years, new attitudes about gay rights, smoking, drinking, guns, animal rights, vegetarianism, etc. have come into the mainstream. But there hasn't really been a strong transformation in other areas.

It's a much more civilized society than it was thirty years ago. Plenty of crazy stuff goes on, but in general, there's an overall improvement in the level of tolerance and understanding in this country, a much broader recognition of the rights of other people, of diversity, of the need to recognize oppressive acts that you yourself have been involved in.

There's no more dramatic illustration of that than the attitude towards the original sin of American society—the elimination of the native population. The founding fathers sometimes condemned it, usually long after their own involvement, but from then to the 1960s, it was hardly mentioned.

When I grew up, we played cowboys and Indians (and I was supposed to be some kind of young radical). My children certainly wouldn't have played like that, and obviously my grandchildren don't.

Looking at the timing, I suspect that a lot of the hysteria about political correctness was whipped up out of frustration over the fact that it wasn't going to be possible, in 1992, to have the kind of 500th anniversary celebration of Columbus' landing in the New World you could have had thirty years earlier. There's much more understanding today of what actually took place.

I'm not saying things are great now, but they are much better, in virtually every area. In the 1700s, the way people treated each other was an unbelievable horror. A century ago, workers' rights in the US were violently repressed.

Even fifty years ago, things were pretty bad. Repression of blacks in the South was obscene. Options for women were highly restricted. There was plenty of upper-class anti-Semitism too.

Harvard had almost no Jewish faculty when I got there about 1950. When my wife and I were looking for a house in the suburbs, we were told by realtors that "we wouldn't be happy" in certain areas we liked. Blacks were of course treated far worse.

The 1890s—the "Gay Nineties"—weren't so gay for the workers in western Pennsylvania. They lived under a brutal tyranny instituted by the great pacifist Andrew Carnegie and the troops he called out in Homestead (and elsewhere).

It wasn't until the '30s, forty years later, that people were even willing to talk about what happened. People who grew up around there tell me that their parents (or grandparents) were afraid to talk about it to the end of their lives.

In 1919 or so, almost thirty years after Homestead, there was a steel strike in western Pennsylvania. [The union activist] Mother Jones [1830–1930], who was then about 90, came to give a talk. Before she could speak, the police dragged her off and threw her into jail. That's pretty rough.

In the 1920s—the "Roaring Twenties"—business control seemed total, and the means used to achieve it could hardly "proceed in anything remotely resembling a democracy," as political scientist Thomas Ferguson pointed out. He was referring to state repression, violence, destruction of unions and harsh management controls.

Yale labor historian David Montgomery, extensively reviewing the same period, wrote that modern America was "created over its workers' protests," with "fierce struggle" in a "most undemocratic America." The 1920s aren't very long ago.

In the early 1960s, the South was a terror state; it's not at all like that now. The beginnings of some kind of commitment to decent medical care for the entire population only go back to the '60s. Concern for environmental protection doesn't really begin until the '70s.

Right now we're trying to defend a minimal health care system; thirty years ago there wasn't a minimal health care system to defend. That's progress.

All those changes took place because of constant, dedicated struggle, which is hard and can look very depressing for long periods. Of course you can always find ways in which these new attitudes have been distorted and turned into techniques of oppression, careerism, self-aggrandize ment and so on. But the overall change is toward greater humanity.

Unfortunately, this trend hasn't touched the central areas of power. In fact, it can be tolerated, even supported, by major institutions, as long as it doesn't get to the heart of the matter—their power and domination over the society, which has actually *increased*. If these new attitudes really started affecting the distribution of power, you'd have some serious struggles.

Disney is a good example of the kind of accommodation you're describing. It exploits Third World labor in Haiti and elsewhere, but domestically it has very liberal policies on gay rights and health care.

It's perfectly consistent for the kind of corporate oligopoly we have to say that we shouldn't discriminate among people. They're all equal— equally lacking in the right to control their own fate, all capable of being passive, apathetic, obedient consumers and workers. The people on top will have greater rights, of course, but they'll be *equally* greater rights—regardless of whether they're black, white, green, gay, heterosexual, men, women, whatever.

You arrived very late for a talk you gave in Vancouver. What were the circumstances?

The event was organized by the British Columbia labor movement. My talk was scheduled for about 7 pm. I should have made it in ample time, but every imaginable thing went wrong with the airlines, and I didn't get there until about 10:30 or 11:00.

To my amazement there were still (what looked like) 800 or 900 people there—they'd been watching documentaries and having discussions. I didn't bother with the talk—it was too late for that—so we just started off with a discussion. It was quite lively, and went on for a couple of hours.

Toward the end of the question-and-answer period, someone asked you about the power of the system and how to change it. You said it's "a very weak system. It looks powerful but could easily be changed." Where do you see the weaknesses?

I see them at every level. We've discussed them earlier, but here's a summary:

- People don't like the system. As mentioned earlier, 95% of Americans think corporations should lower their profits to benefit their workers and the communities they do business in, 70% think businesses have too much power, and more than 80% think that working people don't have enough say in what goes on, that the economic system is inherently unfair, and that the government basically isn't functioning, because it's working for the rich.

- Corporations—the major power system in the West—are chartered by states, and legal mechanisms exist to take away their charters and place them under worker or community control. That would require a democratically organized public, and it hasn't been done for a century. But the rights of corporations were mostly given to them by courts and lawyers, not by legislation, and that power system could erode very quickly.

Of course, the system, once in place, cannot simply be dismantled by legal tinkering. Alternatives have to be constructed within the existing economy, and within the minds of working people and communities. The questions that arise go to the core of socioeconomic organization, the nature of decision-making and control, and the fundamentals of human rights. They are far from trivial.

- Since government is to some extent under public control—at least potentially—it can also be modified.

- About two-thirds of all financial transactions in the globalized economy take place in areas dominated by the US, Japan and Germany. These are all areas where—in principle at least—mechanisms already exist that allow the public to control what happens.

People need organizations and movements to gravitate to.

If people become aware of constructive alternatives, along with even the beginnings of mechanisms to realize those alternatives, positive change could have a lot of support. The current tendencies, many of which are pretty harmful, don't seem to be all that substantial, and there's nothing inevitable about them. That doesn't mean constructive change *will* happen, but the opportunity for it is definitely there.

RESISTANCE

Who knows where the next Rosa Parks [the African-American woman whose refusal to sit in the back of the bus ignited the Montgomery bus boycott in 1955] will sit down and spark a movement?

Rosa Parks is a very courageous and honorable person, but she didn't come out of nowhere. There had been an extensive background of education, organizing and struggle, and she was more or less chosen to do what she did. It's that kind of background that we should be seeking to develop.

Union membership in the US is very low, but it's even lower in France. Yet the support for French general strikes—which shut down cities and, at one point, the whole country—was extraordinarily high. What accounts for that difference?

One factor is the power of business propaganda in the US, which has succeeded, to an unusual extent, in breaking down the relations among people and their sense of support for one another. This is the country where the public relations industry was developed, and where it's still the most sophisticated. It's also the home of the international entertainment industry, whose products are mainly a form of propaganda.

Although there's no such thing as a purely capitalist society (nor could there be), the US is toward the capitalist end. It tends to be more business-run, and spends a huge amount on marketing (which, as I said earlier, is basically an organized form of deceit). A large part of that is advertising, which is tax-deductible, so we all pay for the privilege of being manipulated and controlled.

And of course that's only one aspect of the campaign to "regiment the public mind." Legal barriers against class-based solidarity actions by working people are another device, not found in other industrial democracies, to fragment the general population.

In 1996, Ralph Nader ran for president on the Green Party ticket, and both the Labor Party and the Alliance held founding conventions. The New Party has been running candidates and winning elections. What do you think of all this?

Allowing new options to enter the political system is—in general—a good idea. I think the right way to do it might be the New Party strategy of targeting winnable local elections, backing fusion candidates and—crucially—relating such electoral efforts to ongoing organizing and activism. A labor-based party is a very good idea too.

Since they have basically the same interests, such parties ought to get together—it isn't a good idea to scatter energies and resources that are very slight. A possible step might be to create something like the NDP [New Democratic Party] in Canada or the Workers' Party in Brazil—big organizations that foster and support grassroots activities, bring people together, provide an umbrella under which activities can be carried out and—among other things—take part in the political system, if that turns out to be useful.

That can progress towards something else, but it's not going to overcome the fact that one big business party, with two factions, runs things. We won't break out of that until we democratize the basic structure of our institutions.

As John Dewey put it about seventy years ago, "Politics is the shadow cast on society by big business." As long as you have highly concentrated, unaccountable private power, politics is just going to be a shadow. But you might as well make use of the shadow as much as possible, and use it to try to undermine what's casting the shadow.

Didn't Dewey warn against mere "attenuation of the shadow"?

He said that mere "attenuation of the shadow will not change the substance," which is correct, but it can create the *basis* for undermining the substance. It goes back to the Brazilian rural workers' image I mentioned earlier—expanding the floor of the cage. Eventually you want to dismantle the cage, but expanding the floor of the cage is a step towards that.

It creates different attitudes, different understandings, different forms of participation, different ways for life to be lived, and also yields insight into the limits of existing institutions. That's typically learned by struggle.

All these things are to the good. They only attenuate, that's true, and by themselves they won't overcome, but they're the basis for overcoming. If you can rebuild, reconstitute and strengthen a culture in which social bonds are considered significant, you've made a step towards undermining the control that private and state power exercise over society.

In a cover story in the Nation, Daniel Singer described "the unmistakable attempt by the international financial establishment and [European] governments to [adopt] Reaganomics" and the "striking signs of resistance in Europe" against this. There have been mass demonstrations in France, Germany and Italy, and

250,000 Canadians turned out in Toronto to protest what was going on. That's 1% of the *total* population of Canada—an astonishing figure.

There's been a lot of response all over the place.

Traditionally, campuses have been a major source of resistance. Yet a new study from UCLA says that student activism is at an all-time low, and that interest in government and politics has plummeted. It also states that students' "academic involvement has gone down as well....They're watching more TV." Does that track with your own perceptions?

To say that this is a low point is short-sighted. Is it lower than the 1950s? Is it lower than 1961, when John F. Kennedy sent the Air Force to bomb South Vietnam and you couldn't get a single person to think about it?

When I gave talks on the war in the mid-1960s, we couldn't get anybody to attend. Students weren't interested—except sometimes in attacking the traitors who were condemning government policy. Most of the real and important student activism took place in the late '60s, and it was by no means "traditional."

What about the anti-apartheid movement in the late 1980s?

That was real and important, but it's not all that was happening in the '80s. The Central America solidarity movement was far more deeply rooted in the mainstream of society. Students were involved, but they weren't by any means at the core of it. You found more in churches in places like Arizona and Kansas than in the elite universities.

As for the decline in student activism (and reading, and academic work), that's not students—that's the society. The Robert Putnam study we discussed earlier found about a 50% decline since the '60s in any form of interaction—visiting your neighbor, going to PTA meetings, joining a bowling league. (There's debate about his conclusions, but something of the sort seems to be correct.)

What about the nonaligned movement?

In the 1950s, several Third World leaders tried to establish a form of nonalignment, which decolonization and the conflict between the US and the USSR made possible. By now, that movement has pretty much disappeared, both because of enormous changes in the global economy and because the end of the Cold War eliminated the superpower competition and the deterrent effect of Soviet power, which allowed for a degree of independence. The West doesn't have to pretend anymore that it's interested in helping anybody.

The decline of the nonaligned movement and of Western social democracy are two parts of the same picture. Both reflect the radicalization of the modern socio-economic system, where more and more power is put into the hands of unaccountable institutions that are basically totalitarian (though they happen to be private, and crucially reliant on powerful states).

Is the nonaligned movement completely gone?

As recently as the early 1990s, the South Commission, which represented the governments of nonaligned countries, came out with a very important critique of the antidemocratic, neoliberal model that's being forced on the Third World. (The commission included pretty conservative people, like Indonesia's development minister.)

They published a book that called for a new world order (they introduced the term before George Bush did) based on democracy, justice, development and so on. The book wasn't obscure—it was published by Oxford University Press. I wrote about it, but I couldn't find much else. They subsequently published another book of essays commenting on the first one, and I've never seen a reference to that either.

The South Commission happened to represent most of the world's population, but the story they were telling just isn't one the Western media wanted to hear. So the "new world order" we learned about was Bush's, not the one advocated by the South Commission, which reflects the interests of most of the people of the world.

Back in the '50s, there were Nehru, Nasser, Tito, Nkrumah, Sukarno and others...

All of whom were despised by the US government.

But there was also a period of intellectual ferment in the newly independent countries. I'm thinking of people like Amilcar Cabral [1924–73, leader of the independence struggle in the former Portuguese colony of Guinea in West Africa] and Franz Fanon [1925–61, author of *The Wretched of the Earth,* who fought for Algerian independence]. I don't see much of that right now.

There's still plenty of intellectual ferment, but it doesn't have the enthusiasm and the optimism of those days (although you can hardly call Fanon very optimistic).

It had more of a revolutionary edge back then.

Yes, it did, but remember that since then there's been a period of extreme terror throughout much of the Third World—in which we've played a prominent part—and that's traumatized a lot of people.

The Jesuits of Central America are very courageous people. (Since they're true dissidents within our domains, you hear very little about them here, unless they're murdered. Even their writings are unknown.)

In January 1994, right before the Salvadoran election, they held a conference on the "culture of terror." They said terror has a deeper effect than simply killing a lot of people and frightening a lot of others. They called this deeper effect the "domestication of aspirations"—which basically means that people lose hope. They know that if they try to change things, they're going to get slaughtered, so they just don't try.

The Vatican has had a very harmful impact on all this. It's tried to undermine the progressive thrust of the Latin American church—its "preferential option for the poor" and its attempt to serve as a "voice for the voiceless"—by installing very right-wing bishops. (The *New York Times* had an article on this the other day, but there was a slight omission in it: the role of the US—which is crucial, of course—wasn't mentioned.)

In El Salvador in 1995, the Pope installed as archbishop a Spaniard from the right-wing Opus Dei, who essentially told the poor: *Don't worry about social conditions. If you keep away from sin, everything will be fine in the next life.* This was after the assassination of Archbishop Romero, along with dozens of priests, bishops, nuns and tens of thousands of others, in the brutal war the US ran in the 1980s—a major aim of which was to destroy the Salvadoran Church's concern for the poor. The new archbishop accepted the rank of Brigadier-General from the military, which—he explained—did not "commit errors" as an institution and was now "purified."

Similar things have happened elsewhere. In Indonesia, the Communist Party (PKI) had millions of followers. Even conservative experts on Indonesia recognize that the PKI's strength was based on the fact that it really did represent the interests of poor people. In 1965, General Suharto and his followers in the army presided over the slaughter of hundreds of thousands of landless peasants (and others) and wiped out the PKI.

They went on to compile a world-class record of terror, torture, aggression, massacre and corruption. The Clinton administration has described Suharto as "our kind of guy." Amazingly, quite an impressive popular struggle is still going on in Indonesia, but of course we don't hear much about it.

You once wrote to a mutual friend that when educated classes line up for a parade, people of conscience have three options—they can march in the parade, join the cheering throngs on the sidelines, or speak out against the parade (and, of course, expect to pay the price for doing that).

That's about right. That's been the story for a couple of thousand years or so. Go back to the oldest recorded texts and see what happens to people who didn't march in the parade...like Socrates. Or take the intellectuals described in the Bible (where they're called "prophets").

There were two types of prophets. One type, who flattered the kings and either led the parade or cheered it from the sidelines, were honored and respected. (Much later, they were called false prophets, but not at the time.) Then there were people like Amos, who incidentally insisted that he was not a prophet or the son of one, just a poor shepherd.

True prophets like Amos—"dissident intellectuals," in modern terminology—offered both elevated moral lessons, which the people in power weren't fond of, and geopolitical analyses that usually turned out to be pretty accurate, which the people in power were even less fond of. Naturally, the true prophets were despised, imprisoned, driven into the desert.

The public also hated the true prophets—they didn't want to hear the truth either. Not because they were bad people, but for all the usual reasons—short-term interest, manipulation, dependence on power.

THE MAGIC ANSWER

I often hear the Internet proposed as the one great solution to society's problems.

The Internet should be taken seriously; like other technologies, it has lots of opportunities and lots of dangers. You can't ask, *Is a hammer good or bad?* In the hands of somebody who's building a house, it's good; in the hands of a torturer, it's bad. The Internet is the same. But even used for good, it's obviously not the solution to everything.

When we do something, do we have to have a clear idea about the long-term goal in order to devise a strategy?

We learn by trying. We can't start now, with current understanding, and say, *Okay, let's design a libertarian society.* We have to gain the insight and understanding that allows us to move step-by-step toward that end. Just as in any other aspect of life, as you do more, you learn more. You associate with other people and create organizations, and out of them come new problems, new methods, new strategies.

If somebody can come up with a general, all-purpose strategy, everyone will be delighted, but it hasn't happened in the last couple of thousand years. If Marx had been asked, *What's the strategy for overthrowing capitalism?*, he would have laughed.

Even somebody who was overwhelmingly a tactician, like Lenin, didn't have any such strategy (other than *follow me*). Lenin and Trotsky just adapted strategies to particular circumstances, looking for a way to take state power (which I don't think should be our goal, by the way).

How could there be a general strategy for over-coming authoritarian institutions? I think questions like that are mostly asked by people who don't want to become engaged. When you become engaged, plenty of problems arise that you can work on.

But it's not going to happen by pushing a button. It's going to happen by dedicated, concentrated work that slowly builds up people's understanding and relationships, including one's own, along with support systems and alternative institutions. Then something can happen.

Urvashi Vaid, author of Virtual Equality, *castigates what she calls the "purist left" for waiting for the perfect vision, the one and only answer, as well as a charismatic leader.*

I agree. Not waiting for a charismatic leader, or the perfect and complete answer, is good advice. In fact, if it comes, it will be a disaster, as it always has been.

If something grows out of popular action and participation, it can be healthy. Maybe it won't, but at least it *can* be. There's no other way.

You've always seen top-down strategies and movements as inherently doomed.

They can succeed very well at exactly what they're designed to do—maintain top-down leadership, control and authority. It shouldn't have come as a tremendous surprise to anyone that a vanguard party would end up running a totalitarian state.

Howard Zinn suggests that we need to recognize that real social change takes time. We need to be long-distance runners, not sprinters. What do you think of that?

He's right. It was very striking in parts of the student movement in the '60s. There wasn't an organized, well-established, popular-based left for the students to join, so their leaders were sometimes very young people. They were often very good and decent people, but the perception of many—not all—of them was quite short-range. The idea was, *We'll strike Columbia, close down the buildings for a couple of weeks, and after that we'll have a revolution.*

That's not the way things work. You have to build slowly and ensure that your next step grows out what's already established in people's perceptions and attitudes, their conception of what they want to attain and the circumstances in which it's possible to attain it.

It makes absolutely no sense to expose yourself and others to destruction when you don't have a social base from which you can protect the gains that you've made. That's been found over and over again in guerrilla movements and the like—you just get crushed by the powerful. A lot of the spirit of '68 was like that. It was a disaster for many of the people involved, and it left a sad legacy.

Are you aware of different sorts of responses you get from different audiences?

Over the years, I have noticed a very striking difference between talks I give to more or less elite audiences, and meetings and discussions I have with less privileged people. A while back I was in a town in Massachusetts at a meeting set up by very good local organizers in the urban community—people who were pretty poor, even by world standards. Not long before that, I spent time in the West Bengal countryside. Then I was in Colombia, talking to human rights activists who are working under horrifying conditions.

In places like that, people never ask, *What should I do?* They say, *Here's what I'm doing. What do you think about it?* Maybe they'd like reactions or suggestions, but they're already dealing with the problem. They're not sitting around waiting for a magic answer, which doesn't exist.

When I speak to elite audiences, I constantly get asked, *What's the solution?* If I say obvious things like *Pick your cause and go volunteer for a group that's working on it,* that's never the answer they want. They want some sort of magic key that will solve everything quickly, overwhelmingly and effectively. There are no such solutions. There are only the kind that people are working on in Massachusetts towns, in self-governing villages in India, at the Jesuit Center in Colombia.

People who are actually engaged in dealing with the problems of life, often under extreme repression and very harsh conditions, sometimes just give up. You can find that too. But many keep struggling effectively and bring about changes.

That's been true in our own history. Right now we're facing real problems, like protecting the limited level of public medical care, the Social Security system, environmental rights, workers' rights. But you don't have to go very far back to get to the time when people were trying to *gain* those rights. That's a big change. It's a lot better to be protecting something than trying to get it for the first time.

These rights are the result of popular engagement and struggle. If there's another way to achieve them, it's been kept a dark secret. But privileged audiences often don't want to hear that. They want a quick answer that will get the job done fast.

MANUFACTURING DISSENT

Michael Moore made a documentary film called *Roger and Me,* and produced a television series called *TV Nation.* In his book *Downsize This!,* he says that what turns people off about the left is that it's boring, it whines too much, it's too negative. Anything to that?

I don't think Howard Zinn, say, whines too much and turns people off, but there are probably other people who do. To the extent that that's true, it's a problem they should overcome.

Take the example of the media group in Brazil we discussed earlier, which presented television skits that turned people off because they were boring and full of jargon. This group went back to the people and let them produce the stuff themselves, simply providing technical assistance. That second set of programs wasn't boring and didn't turn people off.

That's exactly the correct approach. People who write about the responsibility of intellectuals should *assume* that responsibility and go out and work with people, provide them whatever help you can, learn from them.

You've observed grassroots movements in places like India, Brazil and Argentina. Can we learn anything from them?

Those are very vibrant, dynamic societies, with huge problems and lots going on. But I think they're also trapped by delusions like, *We've got this terrible foreign debt. We've got to minimize the state.* They've got to understand that they don't have any debt—just as *we* have to understand that corporations are illegitimate private tyrannies.

You've got to free yourself intellectually, and you can't do it alone—you liberate yourself through participation with others, just as you learn things in science by interacting with others. Popular organizations and umbrella groups help create a basis for this.

Is that enough to bring about serious changes?

It's hard to say. We have all sorts of advantages that they don't have—like enormous wealth, for instance. We also have a unique advantage—there's no superpower standing over us. We *are* the superpower. That makes a huge difference.

But when you come back from the Third World to the West—the US in particular—you're struck by the narrowing of thought and understanding, the limited nature of legitimate discussion, the separation of people from each other. It's startling how stultifying it feels, since our opportunities are so vastly greater here.

Do you have any ideas on how we can move from preaching to the choir, to people that already agree with us? This seems to be a major problem.

First of all, as we've discussed a couple of times already, a large majority already does agree with these ideas. The question is, how to turn those general attitudes into real understanding and constructive actions. The answer is, by organizing to do so.

Whenever I—or anybody—gives a talk, it's because some group has set it up. I can't just show up in Kansas City and say, *I'm going to give a talk*—nobody would come. But if a group there organizes it, people will come from all over the place, and maybe that will help the organizers, and others, to get together and to proceed more effectively.

This all goes back to the same thing: If people dedicate themselves to organizing and activism, we'll gain access to broader and broader audiences.

As you know, I do a one-hour radio program every week. It's pretty effectively locked out of the Boston-to-Miami corridor, but in the West—in Montana, Colorado, New Mexico, and places like that—it's much easier to get it on the air.

It doesn't matter much to the power centers what people are talking about in Laramie, Wyoming. The East Coast is where most of the decisions get made, so that's what has to be kept under tight doctrinal control.

But we can't just blame the people in power. We aren't making use of the possibilities we have.

Take Cambridge, where we're sitting now. Like other towns, it has a community cable television station (the communications act requires that cable companies provide them). I've been there. I'm not much of a techie, but even I could see that it has pretty good equipment. It's available to the public, but is it used by anyone?

The one time I was on that station, the program was so crazy I almost walked off. What would happen if you had lively, quality local cable TV? The commercial channels would have to respond to that. They might try to stop it or undercut it or co-opt it, but they'd have to do something if there got to be enough of it. So would NPR. They can't completely disregard what's happening in their communities.

So that's one resource that isn't being used the way it could be. In the slums of Rio, they'd be delighted if they had cable television stations that the people could use. We have them and we're not using them effectively.

Cassette tapes are one mechanism to disseminate this information. They're easy to duplicate and pass around. The Iranian revolution was called the first cassette revolution.

There are lots of opportunities. Compared with people in other countries, our resources and options are so enormous that we can only blame ourselves for not doing more.

In Elaine Briére's documentary film on East Timor, *Bitter Paradise,* you say, "The press isn't in the business of letting people know how power works. It would be crazy to expect that....They're part of the power system—

why should they expose it?" Given that, is there any point in sending op-ed pieces to newspapers, writing letters to the editor, making phone calls?

They're all very good things to do. Our system is much more flexible and fluid than a real tyranny, and even a real tyranny isn't immune to public pressures. Every one of these openings should be exploited, in all sorts of ways.

When you get away from the really top, agenda-setting media, there are plenty of opportunities. It isn't just a matter of writing op-eds and making telephone calls, but insisting, by all kinds of public pressures, that there be openings to your point of view.

There are understandable institutional reasons why the media are so deeply indoctrinated and hard to penetrate, but it's not graven in stone. In fact, the same factors that make it so rigid also make it rich in ways to overcome that rigidity. But you have to *do* something—you can't just sit around waiting for a savior.

Another approach is creating alternative media, which may well have the effect of opening up the major media. That's often been done.

But you don't see getting the occasional op-ed piece published as a substitute for a truly independent, democratic media.

It's not a substitute—it's a step towards it. These things interact.

You're often introduced as someone who speaks truth to power, but I believe you take issue with that Quaker slogan.

The Quakers you're referring to are very honest and decent, and some of the most courageous people I've ever known. We've been through a lot together, gone to jail together, and we're friends. But—as I've told them plenty of times—I don't like that slogan.

Speaking truth to power makes no sense. There's no point in speaking the truth to Henry Kissinger—he knows it already. Instead, speak truth to the *powerless*—or, better, *with* the powerless. Then they'll *act* to dismantle illegitimate power.

A Canadian journal called *Outlook* ran an article on the talk you gave in Vancouver. It concluded with quotes from people leaving the hall: *Well, he certainly left me depressed.* And: *I'm more upset than I was before I came.* And on and on. Is there any way to change that?

I've heard that a lot, and I understand why. I feel that it's none of my business to tell people what they ought to do—that's for them to figure out. I don't even know what *I* ought to do.

So I just try to describe as best I can what I think is happening. When you look at that, it's not very pretty, and if you extrapolate it into the future, it's very ugly.

But the point is—and it's my fault if I don't make this clear—*it's not inevitable.* The future can be changed. But we can't change things unless we at least begin to understand them.

We've had plenty of successes; they're cumulative, and they lead us to new peaks to climb. We've also had plenty of failures. Nobody ever said it was going to be easy.

SOME ORGANIZATIONS WORTH SUPPORTING

The 160 US and Canadian groups listed in this section were suggested by Noam Chomsky, Jane Maxwell, Chris Rosene, Davida Coady, Gar Smith, Susan McCallister, David Barsamian, Sheila Katz, Todd Jailer, Maya Shaw, Naomi Mudge, Adrienne Fugh-Berman, Elaine Brière, Greg Bates and myself. Janee Campagne and I checked and updated the contact information.

I've grouped the organizations into the following rough categories:

- affordable housing
- anti-war and economic conversion
- Asia
- church groups (multi-issue)
- civil rights
- community organizing
- Cuba
- economic justice (domestic)
- environmental
- funding groups
- general and miscellaneous
- health and reproductive rights
- human rights
- labor
- Latin America
- media and communications
- Middle East
- political parties and groups
- research
- Third World development
- women's issues

It's unlikely that any of us who suggested organizations would agree with everyone else's choices, so please don't assail us with complaints about which groups are—or aren't—on the list.

There are *many, many* other worthwhile groups—particularly small, local ones. One way to find them is to ask any of the regional funding organizations on pp. 163–64 which groups they support. Many of the national organizations below also have local branches.

There's a list of good sources for current information on pp. 170 and 171. The organizations that publish these periodicals (websites, etc.) should also be considered part of this list. *Arthur Naiman*

AFFORDABLE HOUSING

Also see *Community organiz.*

Fund for an Open Society
311 S Juniper, Suite 400
Philadelphia PA 19107
215 735 6915

Habitat for Humanity
322 W Lamar St
Americus GA 31709
912 924 6935j170

South Shore Bank
7054 S Jeffery Blvd
Chicago IL 60649
800 669 7725

ANTI-WAR & ECONOMIC CONVERSION

Center for Defense Information
1779 Massachusetts NW
Washington DC 20036
202 332 0600; f: 462 4559

Center for Economic Conversion
222 View St
Mountain View CA 94041
650 968 8798

Central Committee for Conscientious Objectors
West: 655 Sutter, Suite 514
San Francisco CA 94102
415 474 3002

CCC0 East: 1515 Cherry St
Philadelphia PA 19102
215 563 8787

Livermore Conversion Project
Box 31835, Oakland CA
94604 • 510 832 4347

National Commission for Economic Conversion and Disarmament
733 15th St NW, Suite 1020
Washington DC 20005
202 234 9382 x214
www.webcom.com/ncecd

Nevada Desert Experience
Box 4487, Las Vegas NV
89127 • 702 648 2798

War Resisters League
339 Lafayette St, New York
NY 10012 • 212 228 0450

ASIA

Also see *Third World devel.*

Burma Project
400 W 59th St, 4th floor
New York NY 10019
212 548 0632, f: 548 4655
www.soros.org/burma.html

Canada Asia Working Group
947 Queen St E, Suite 213
Toronto ON, M4M 1J4
Canada
416 465 8826, f: 463 8826

Canadian Action for Indonesia/East Timor
Box 562, Station P, Toronto ON, M5S 2T1 Canada
416 531 5850, f: 588 5556

East Timor Action Network
Box 1182
White Plains NY 10602
914 428 7299, f: 428 7383
etan-us@igc.org

East Timor Religious Outreach
1600 Clay St
San Francisco CA 94109
415 474 6219

Free Burma Coalition
c/o Dept. of Curriculum & Instruction, University of Wisconsin, 225 N Mills St, Madison WI 53706
608 827 7734
justfree@ix.netcom.com

CHURCH GROUPS
(MULTI-ISSUE)

American Friends Service Committee (Quakers)
1501 Cherry St
Philadelphia PA 19102
215 241 7000

Anglican Church of Canada
600 Jarvis St, Toronto ON M4Y 2J6 Canada
416 924 9192

Canadian Catholic Organ. for Development and Peace
5633 Sherbrooke St E
Montréal, Québec H1N 1A3 Canada
514 257 8711

Maryknoll Mission Association of the Faithful
Box 307
Maryknoll NY 10545
914 762 6364

Mennonite Central Committee
21 S 12th St or Box 500, Akron PA 17501
717 859 1151

National Council of Churches
475 Riverside Dr, New York NY 10115 • 212 870 2511

Unitarian-Universalist Assn.
25 Beacon St, Boston MA 02108 • 617 742 2100

United Church of Canada
3250 Bloor St W, Suite 300, Etobicoke ON, M8X 2Y4 Canada • *www.uccan.org*
416 231 5931, f: 232 6004

CIVIL RIGHTS

Americans United for the Separation of Church and State • 1816 Jefferson Pl NW, Washington DC 20036 • 202 466 3234, f: 466 2587 • *www.au.org*

American Civil Liberties Union
125 Broad St, New York NY 10004 • 212 549 2500

Asian Law Caucus
720 Market St, Suite 500
San Francisco CA 94102
415 391 1655

Center for Constitutional Rights
666 Broadway, 7th floor
New York NY 10012
212 614 6464, f: 614 6499

Disability Rights Advocates
1999 Harrison St, Suite 1760
Oakland CA 94612
510 451 8644

Drug Policy Foundation
4455 Connecticut Ave NW, Suite B-500, Washington DC 20008 • 202 537 5005

MALDEF (Mexican-American Legal Defense and Education Fund)
634 S Spring St
Los Angeles CA 90014
213 629 2512

NAACP (National Association for the Advancement of Colored People)
4805 Mount Hope Dr
Baltimore MD 21215
410 358 8900

National Gay and Lesbian Task Force
2320 17th St NW
Washington DC 20009
202 332 6483

National Urban League
120 Wall St, 8th floor
New York NY 10005
212 558 5300

Native American Rights Fund
1506 Broadway
Boulder CO 80302
303 447 8760

NORML (National Organization for the Reform of Marijuana Laws)
1001 Connecticut Ave NW, #710, Washington DC 20036 • 202 483 5500

Northern California Coalition for Immigrant Rights
995 Market St, Suite 1108
San Francisco CA 94103
415 243 8215, f: 243 8628
nccir@igc.org

People for the American Way
2000 M St NW, Suite 400
Washington DC 20036
202 467 4999, f: 293 2672
www.pfaw.org

COMMUNITY ORGANIZING

ACORN (Association of Community Organizations for Reform Now)
117 W Harrison St, Suite 200
Chicago IL 60605
800 327 4429
www.acorn.org/community

Center for Third World Organizing
1218 E 21st St
Oakland CA 94606
510 533 7583

Highlander Research and Education Center
1959 Highlander Way
New Market TN 37820
615 933 3443

PUEBLO
132 E 12th St
Oakland CA 94606
510 452 2010

CUBA

Also see *Third World devel.*

Disarm Education Fund/ Cuban Medical Project
36 E 12th St
New York NY 10003
212 475 3232

International Peace for Cuba Appeal
39 W 14th St, Suite 206
New York NY 10011
212 633 6646
Also: San Francisco:
415 821 6545

US+Cuba Medical Project
One Union Sq W, Suite 211
New York NY 10003
212 727 3247

ECONOMIC JUSTICE
(DOMESTIC)

Also see *Anti-war* and *economic conversion*.

Center for Ethics and Economic Policy
2512 9th St #3
Berkeley CA 94710
510 549 9931, f: 549 9995

Council of Canadians
151 Slater St S502, Ottawa
ON, K1P 5H3 Canada
613 233 2773

Ecumenical Council for Economic Justice (ECEJ)
947 Queen St E, Suite 208
Toronto M4M 1J9 Canada
416 462 1613, f: 463 5569

United for a Fair Economy
37 Temple Place, 5th floor
Boston MA 02111
617 423 2148 • *www.stw.org*

ENVIRONMENTAL

Alliance for a Paving Moratorium
Box 4347, Arcata CA 95521
707 826 7775

Canadian Environmental Law Association
517 College St, Suite 401
Toronto ON, M6G 4A2
Canada • 416 960 2284

Center for Biological Diversity
Box 710, Tucson AZ 85702
520 623 5252, f: -9797
www.sw-center.org

Citizens' Clearinghouse for Hazardous Wastes
Box 6806, Falls Church VA
22040 • 703 237 2249

Earth First!
Box 1415, Eugene OR 97440
541 344 8004

Earth Island Institute
300 Broadway, Suite 28
San Francisco CA 94133
415 788 3666, f: 788 7324
www.earthisland.org

Earthjustice Legal Defense Fund
180 Montgomery St, #1400
San Francsico CA 94104
415 627 6700, f: 627 6740

Friends of the Earth
218 D St SE
Washington DC 20003
202 544 2600

Greenaction
Box 249
San Francisco CA 94117
415 566 3475

Indigenous Environmental Network
Box 485, Bemidji MN 56619
218 751 4967

PEG (Political Ecology Group)
965 Misson St, Suite 218
San Francisco CA 94103
415 777 3488
www.igc.org/peg

Pesticide Action Network
North American Regional Ctr
116 New Montgomery, # 810
San Francisco CA 94105
415 541 9140, f; 541 9253

FUNDING GROUPS

The Funding Exchange is a national network office for progressive funds. The other funds listed all have a regional focus, except for Resist and the Rosenberg Fund.

Funding Exchange
666 Broadway, Suite 500
New York NY 10012
212 529 5300, f: 982 9272
www.fex.org/fxc.html

Appalachian Community Fund
517 Union Ave, Suite 206
Knoxville TN 37902
423 523 5783, f: 523 1896

Bread and Roses Community Fund
1500 Walnut St, Suite 1305
Philadelphia PA 19102
215 731 1107

Chinook Fund
2418 W 32nd Ave
Denver CO 80211
303 455 6905

Crossroads Fund
3411 W Diversey Ave, #20
Chicago IL 60647
773 227 7676

Fund for Santa Barbara
735 State St, Suite 211
Santa Barbara CA 93101
805 962 9164, f: 965 0217

Fund for Southern Communities
547 Ponce de Leon Ave NE
Atlanta GA 30308
404 876 4147, f: 876 3453

Haymarket People's Fund
42 Seaverns Ave
Jamaica Plain MA 02130
617 522 7676

Headwaters Fund
122 W Franklin Ave, #518
Minneapolis MN 55404
612 879 0602

Liberty Hill Foundation
1316 Third St Promenade, #B-4
Santa Monica CA 90401
310 458 1450, f: 451 4283

McKenzie River Gathering Foundation
3558 SE Hawthorne
Portland OR 97214
503 233 0271

North Star Fund
305 7th Ave, 5th floor
New York NY 10001
212 620 9110

People's Fund
1325 Nuuanu Ave
Honolulu HI 96817
808 526 2441
www.fex.org,
peoples@lava.net

Resist
259 Elm St, Suite 201
Somerville MA 02144
617 623 5110
www.resistinc.org

Rosenberg Fund for Children
1145 Main St, Suite 408
Springfield MA 01103
413 739 9020

Three Rivers Community Fund
100 N Braddock Ave, #207
Pittsburgh PA 15208
412 243 9250

Vanguard Public Foundation
383 Rhode Island, Suite 301
San Francisco CA 94103
415 487 2111

Wisconsin Community Fund
122 State St, Suite 507A
Madison WI 53703
608 251 6834

GENERAL AND MISC.

Center for Living Democracy
Box 8187, Brattleboro VT
05304, or 289 Fox Farm
Rd, Brattleboro VT 05301
802 254 1234

Gray Panthers
2025 Pennsylvania Ave NW,
Suite 821
Washington DC 20006
202 466 3132

SOME ORGANIZATIONS WORTH SUPPORTING

INFACT
256 Hanover St
Boston MA 02113
617 742 4583, f: 397 0191
www.infact.org

Nader organizations
Scores of organizations affiliated with or recommended by Ralph Nader are listed at *www.essential.org*

Neighbor to Neighbor Action Fund
1611 Telegraph Ave, #1111
Oakland CA 94612
800 366 8289 or 510 419 0101 x218, f: 419 0202

Open Society Institute/ Soros Foundations Network
www.soros.org

Physicians for Social Responsibility
1101 14th St NW, Suite 700
Washington DC 20005
202 898 0150, f: 898 0172
www.psr.org
psrnatl@psr.org

Prison Moritorium Project
180 Varick St, 12th floor
New York NY 10014
212 727 8610

Public Citizen
1600 20th St NW
Washington DC 20009
202 588 1000

Quixote Center
Box 5206
Hyattsville MD 20782
301 699 0042

Women's International League for Peace and Freedom
1213 Race St
Philadelphia PA 19107
215 563 7110

HEALTH AND REPRODUCTIVE RIGHTS
Also see *Cuba* and *Latin America*.

Advocates for Youth
1025 Vermont Ave NW, Suite 200, Washington DC 20005 • 202 347 5700

Boston Women's Health Book Collective
Box 192, Somerville MA 02144 • 617 625 0277
www.ourbodiesourselves.org

Hesperian Foundation
Box 11577
Berkeley CA 94712
510 845 1447 or -4507
f: 510 845 9141 or -0539

NARAL (National Abortion and Reproductive Rights Action League)
1156 15th St NW, Suite 700
Washington DC 20005
202 973 3060

National Women's Health Network
514 Tenth St NW, Suite 400
Washington DC 20004
202 347 1140, f: 347 1168

Partners in Health
113 River St, Cambridge MA 02139 • 617 661 4564

Planned Parenthood
810 Seventh Ave
New York NY 10019
212 541 7800

Seva Foundation
1786 Fifth St, Berkeley CA 94710 • 510 845 7382, f: 845 7410 • *www.seva.org*
admin@seva.org
Canada: 2678 W Broadway, Suite 200, Vancouver BC, V6K 2G3
604 733 4284, f: 733 4292

Women's Health Rights Coalition
558 Capp St
San Francisco CA 94110
415 647 2697

HUMAN RIGHTS

Also see *Asia, Latin America* and *Middle East.*

Amnesty International USA
322 Eighth Ave
New York NY 10001
212 807 8400

Human Rights Watch
(incl. Americas Watch, Africa Watch, Asia Watch, etc.)
350 Fifth Ave, 34th floor
New York NY 10118
212 290 4700

Physicians for Human Rights
100 Boylston St, Suite 702
Boston MA 02116
617 695 0041

LABOR

Coalition of Labor Union Women
1126 16th St NW
Washington DC 20036
202 466 4610

Labor Party
Box 53177
Washington DC 20009
202 234 5190

LATIN AMERICA

Also see *Cuba* and *Third World development.*

CISPES (Committee in Solidarity with the People of El Salvador)
19 W 21st St, Suite 502
New York NY 10010
212 229 1290
www.cispes.org

CHRIA (Committee for Health Rights in the Americas)
474 Valencia St, Suite 120
San Francisco CA 94131
415 431 7760

Global Exchange
2017 Mission, Suite 303
San Francisco CA 94110
415 255 7296, f: 255 7498
www.globalexchange.org

Guatemala Partners
1830 Connecticut Ave NW
Washington DC 20009
202 783 1123

GNIB (Guatemala News and Information Bureau)
3181 Mission St, Box 12
San Francisco CA 94110
415 826 3593; f: same #
gnib@igc.org

InterChurch Committee for Human Rights in Latin America (ICCHRLA)
129 St Clair Ave W, Toronto
ON M4V 1N9, Canada
416 921 0801, f: 921 3843

Inter-Hemispheric Education Resource Center
Box 4506
Albuquerque NM 87196
505 842 8288

MADRE
121 W 27th St, Suite 301
New York NY 10001
212 627 0444

Mexico Solidarity Network
4934 N Springfield
Chicago IL 60625
773 583 7728
alex2051@xsite.net

NACLA (North American Congress on Latin America)
475 Riverside Dr, Suite 454
New York NY 10115
212 870 3146

Nicaragua Network
1247 E St SE, Washington
DC 20003 • 202 544 9355

NISGUA (Network in
Solidarity with the
People of Guatemala)
1830 Connecticut Ave NW
Washington DC 20009
202 518 7638, f: 223 8221
nisgua@igc.org

Office of the Americas
8124 W Third St, Suite 202
Los Angeles CA 90048
213 852 9808

**Resource Center of the
Americas**
317 17th Ave SE
Minneapolis MN 55404
612 627 9445

San Carlos Foundation
1065 Creston Rd
Berkeley CA 94708
510 525 3787

Witness for Peace
1229 15th St NW
Washington DC 20005
202 588 1471, f: 588 1472
www.igc.org/wfp

WOLA (Washington Office
on Latin America)
1630 Connecticut Ave NW,
2nd floor
Washington DC 20009
202 797 2171, f: 797 2172
www.wola.org

MEDIA AND COMMUNICATIONS

Alternative Radio
See p. 191.

**Center for Investigative
Reporting**
500 Howard St, Suite 206
San Francisco 94105
415 543 1200, f: 543 8311

Deep Dish TV
339 Lafayette St
New York NY 10012
212 473 8933

FAIR (Fairness and
Accuracy in Reporting)
130 W 25th St, 8th floor
New York NY 10001
212 633 6700
www.fair.org

Free Speech TV
Box 6060
Boulder CO 80306
303 442 5693

Friends of Free Speech Radio
905 Parker St
Berkeley CA 94710
510 548 0542
www.savepacifica.net

Global Vision
1600 Broadway, Suite 700
New York NY 10019
212 246 0202

IGC (Institute for Global
Communications)
Box 29904
San Francisco CA 94129
415 561 6100, f: -6101
www.igc.org
support@igc.apc.org

**Institute for Public
Accuracy**
915 National Press Building
Washington DC 20045
202 347 0020
www.accuracy.org
institute@igc.org

National Radio Project
1714 Franklin St, Suite 311
Oakland CA 94612
510 251 1332

Public Media Center
466 Green St, Suite 300
San Francisco CA 94133
415 434 1403

MIDDLE EAST

Jewish Peace Lobby
8604 Second Ave, Suite 317
Silver Spring MD 20910
301 589 8764

Middle East Children's Alliance
905 Parker St
Berkeley CA 94710
510 548 0542

Search for Justice and Equality in Palestine/Israel
Box 3452
Framingham MA 01705
508 877 2611

POLITICAL PARTIES AND GROUPS

Also see *Labor.*

The Alliance
Box 683, Lincoln MA 01773
781 259 9395, f: 259 0404
www.eal.com/alliance

Democratic Socialists of America
180 Varick St, 12th floor
New York NY 10014
212 727 8610

Green Party USA
Box 1406
Chicago, Illinois 60690
866 GREENS2
www.greenparty.org

New Democratic Party
81 Metcalfe St, #900, Ottawa
ON K1P 6K7 Canada
613 236 3613, f: 230 9950
www.ndp.ca

New Party
88 Third Ave, Suite 313
Brooklyn NY 11217
718 246 3713, 800 200 1294

RESEARCH

Data Center
1904 Franklin St, Suite 900
Oakland CA 94612
510 835 4692

Institute for Policy Studies
733 15th St NW, Suite 1020
Washington DC 20005
202 234 9382

Political Resarch Associates
120 Beacon St, Suite 202
Somerville MA 02143
617 661 9313, f: 661 0059
www.igc.org/pra

THIRD WORLD DEVELOPMENT

Also see *Asia, Cuba*
and *Latin America.*

CCIC (Canadian Council for International Cooperation)
1 Nicholas St, Suite 300
Ottawa ON, K1N 7B7
Canada
613 241 7007

Center for International Policy
1755 Massachusetts Ave
NW, Suite 312
Washington DC 20036
202 232 3317

SOME ORGANIZATIONS WORTH SUPPORTING

The Development Gap for Alternative Policies
927 15th St NW, 4th floor
Washington DC 20005
202 898 1566, f: 898 1612
www.igc.org/dgap/index.html

Fifty Years is Enough Network
1247 E St SE
Washington DC 20003
202 463 2265
www.50years.org

Food First (Institute for Food and Development Policy)
398 60th St
Oakland CA 94618
510 654 4400

Grassroots International
48 Grove St
Somerville MA 02144
617 628 1664, f: -4737
grassroots@igc.org

Inter Pares
58 Arthur St, Ottawa ON
K1R 7B9 Canada
613 563 4801

Maquila Solidarity Network
606 Shaw St, Toronto ON
M6G 3L6, Canada
416 532 8584, f: 532 7688
www.web.net/~msn

Oxfam America
26 West St
Boston MA 02111
617 482 1211

Oxfam Canada
294 Albert St, Suite 300
Ottawa ON, K1P6E6 Canada
613 237 5236

Results
440 First St NW, Suite 450
Washington DC 20001
202 783 7100

World Neighbors
800 242 6387
www.wn.org

WOMEN'S ISSUES

Also see *Health and reproductive rights, Latin America* and *Labor.*

Ms. Foundation
120 Wall St, 33rd floor
New York, NY 10005
212 742 2300

9to5, National Association of Working Women
23 W Wisconsin Ave, #900
Milwaukee WI 53203
414 274 0925

NOW (Nat'l Organization of Women) **Legal Defense and Education Fund**
99 Hudson St, 12th floor
New York NY 10013
212 925 6635

RAINBO (Research Action Information Network for Bodily Integrity of Women)
915 Broadway, Suite 1109
New York NY 10010
212 477 3318, f: 477 4154

WOW (Wider Opportunities for Women)
815 15th St NW, Suite 916
Washington DC 20005
202 638 3143

SOURCES FOR CURRENT INFORMATION

The 31 magazines, newsletters and websites listed below typically provide good, up-to-date information and analysis. As you'd expect, many of the organizations in the previous section also publish useful materials and have valuable websites, so look there too, both under the categories you're interested in and also under Media and Communications). *AN*

GENERAL NEWS

Consortium for Independent Journalism
222 Wilson Blvd, #102-231
Arlington VA 22201
800 738 1812, 703 920 1802
www.consortiumnews.com

CounterPunch
Box 18675, Washington DC
20036 • 202 986 3665

Covert Action Quarterly
1500 Massachusetts Ave
NW, Suite 732
Washington DC 20005
202 331 9763

iF
See *Consortium for Independent Journalism* above.

In These Times
2040 N Milwaukee Ave
Chicago IL 60647
800 827 0270
www.inthesetimes.com

The Nation
33 Irving Pl, NY, NY 10003
212 209 5400
www.TheNation.com

The Progressive
409 E Main St
Madison WI 53703
608 257 4626

Z
18 Millfield St
Woods Hole MA 02543
508 548 9063

CORPORATE CRIME & ECONOMIC ISSUES

Corporate Crime Reporter
1209 National Press Bldg
Washington DC 20045
202 737 1680

Corporate Watch
www.corpwatch.org
Box 29344
San Francisco CA 94129
415 561 6567

Dollars and Sense
One Summer St
Somerville MA 02143
617 628 8411 (9–5 ET)
www.igc.org/dollars
dollars@igc.org

Left Business Observer
250 W 85th St
New York NY 10024
212 874 4020, f: 874 3137
dhenwood@panix.com

Multinational Monitor
1530 P St NW
Washington DC 20005
202 387 8030, f: 234 5176
monitor@essential.org

SOURCES FOR CURRENT INFORMATION

ENVIRONMENTAL

Earth Island Journal
See *Earth Island Institute* on p. 163

Econet
www.igc.org/igc/econet

Green Pages
Co-op America
1612 K St NW, #600
Washington DC 20006
800 584 7336 or
202 872 5307, f: 331 8166
www.greenpages.org

INTERNATIONAL

Middle East Report
MERIP (Middle East Research
& Information Project)
1500 Massachusetts Ave,
Suite 119
Washington DC 20009
202 223 3677, f: 223 3604
www.merip.org

NACLA Report on the Americas – see *NACLA* on p. 166

The New Internationalist
1011 Bloor St W, Suite 300
Toronto ON M6H 1M1
Canada • 416 588 6478

Nicaragua Solidarity Network Weekly News Update on the Americas
339 Lafayette St
New York NY 10012
212 674 9499

LABOR

Labornet
www.igc.org/igc/labornet

Labor Notes
7435 Michigan Ave
Detroit MI 48210
313 842 6262, f: 842 0227
www.labornotes.org

Libertarian Labor Review
Box 2824
Champaign IL 61825
http://flag.blackened.net/llr

Working USA
M.E. Sharpe, 80 Business Pk
Dr, Armonk NY 10504
201 839 1133, f: 839 2417

ANALYTICAL JOURNALS

Against the Current
c/o Center for Changes
7012 Michigan Ave
Detroit MI 48210
313 841 0160

Monthly Review
122 W 27th St, 10th floor
New York NY 10001
212 691 2555, f: 727 3676
www.monthlyreview.org

MISCELLANEOUS

Conflictnet
www.igc.org/igc/conflictnet

Extra! – See *FAIR* on p. 167

Peacenet
www.igc.org/igc/peacenet

Prison Legal News
2400 NW 80th St, #148
Seattle WA 98117
561 547 9716
www.prisonlegalnews.org

Womensnet
www.igc.org/igc/womensnet

NOTES

Citations for the facts in this book are listed below by **page number/topic**. Full information is provided the first time a book is cited; after that, just the title or author(s) are given. "My" means "Chomsky's."   *AN*

7–8/Madison and Jay quotes: See my *Power and Prospects,* chap. 5 (South End, 1996). For more detail and a fuller discussion, see my "'Consent without Consent': Reflections on the Theory and Practice of Democracy," *Cleveland State Law Review* 44.4, 1996.

9/de Tocqueville: *Democracy in America,* vol. 2, chap. 20.

14/Andreas quote: Dan Carney, *Mother Jones,* 12/95.

14/UNDP quote: *Human Development Report 1997,* p. 86 (Oxford Univ. Press, 1997).

14/100 largest transnationals: Winfried Ruigrok & Rob van Tulder, *The Logic of International Restructuring* (Routledge, 1995).

15/*Boston Globe* article: Peter Gosselin, 2/4/97.

15/Japanese semiconductor consortium: Andrew Pollack, "Tokyo Steps In to Help Fund Companies' High-Tech Research," *New York Times* News Service, *International Herald Tribune,* 11/19/86.

19–20/Fidelity: John Cogan, *New York Times;* Gary Putka, *Wall Street Journal;* both 12/14/95. Charles Stein, "Fund firm's tax relief gets green light," *Boston Globe,* 7/31/96.

20/Raytheon: Aaron Zitner, "Debate over Raytheon aid," *Boston Globe,* 4/12/95. Doris Sue Wong, "Business tax cut narrowed," *Boston Globe,* 10/31/95.

27/"subjugation of labor": John Liscio, *Barron's,* 4/15/96.

29–30/Sanders' op-ed: "Balance the Budget—But Do It Fairly," *Boston Globe,* 2/6/97.

30–32/Boeing, etc: Adam Bryant, "Company Loses Bid on Huge Contract for the Pentagon," *NY Times,* 11/17/96; "Behind McDonnell Loss, New Military Reality," *NY Times,* and "Military Contracting Enters a New Era," *TimesFax* (for business customers mainly), 11/18/96.

35–36/foreign operations of US businesses: Department of Commerce, *Survey of Current Business,* 11/96 and 12/96.

36/narco-money & US banks: Apolinar Biaz-Callejas (of the Latin American Association for Human Rights and the Andean Commission of Jurists), *Excelsior* (Mexico), 10/14/94.

37/OSHA under Reagan & Bush: *Business Week,* 5/23/94.

39–40/Webb articles: *San Jose Mercury News,* 8/18–20/96. **His book:** *Dark Alliance* (Seven Stories, 1998).

40/McCoy on drug traffic: Alfred W. McCoy, *The Politics of Heroin in Southeast Asia* (Harper & Row, 1972); *The Politics of Heroin* (Lawrence Hill, 1991).

41/five news filters: "(1) the size, concentrated ownership, owner wealth and profit orientation of the dominant mass-media firms; (2) advertising as the primary income source of the mass media; (3) the reliance of the media on information provided by government, business, and 'experts' funded and approved by these primary sources and agents of power; (4) 'flak' as a means of disciplining the media; and (5) 'anticommunism' as a national religion and control mechanism." Edward S. Herman & Noam Chomsky, *Manufacturing Consent,* p. 2 (Pantheon, 1988).

46–48/Lewis quotes: *New York Times,* 6/7/96. For a discussion of these and many similar comments, see my *Towards a New Cold War,* pp. 144–45 and note 11 (Pantheon, 1982).

48–51/McChesney book:*Telecommunications, Mass Media and Democracy* (Oxford Univ. Press, 1993).

50–51/labor newspapers: Elizabeth Fones-Wolf, *Selling Free Enterprise* (Univ. of Illinois Press, 1995).

51–52/NAFTA winners: Thomas Lueck, *New York Times,* 11/18/93.

52/Putnam article: *The American Prospect,* Winter 1996.

56/Brazilian "economic miracle": Jan Black, *US Penetration of Brazil* (Univ. of Pennsylvania Press, 1977).

61–62/*Business Week* poll: 2/19/96

63/Brady: See, for example, *Business as a System of Power* (Columbia Univ. Press, 1943). Some quotes appear in my *Power and Prospects,* chap. 4.

65–66/Eastern vs. Western European workers: For citations and further discussion, see my *World Orders, Old and New,* chap. 2 (Columbia Univ. Press, 1994, 1996).

68/Owens' & Nye's article: *Foreign Affairs,* Spring 1996.

69/"to regiment the public mind…": Edward Bernays, *Propaganda* (1928).

72/aerospace mergers: See Patrick Sloyan, "Layoff Payoff: Tax Dollars to Enrich Merger Bosses," *Newsday,* 3/17/95. Also his "Sweet Deal from Pentagon," *Newsday,* 6/30/94, which reports a $60-million payoff to Martin Marietta to acquire a rival firm.

73/transnational bailouts: Ruigrock and van Tulder.

73/international financial transactions: Paul Hirst and Grahame Thompson, *Globalization in Question* (Polity, 1996). Figures range from 60% of the flow of foreign direct investment (FDI) to 70% of exports and 75% of total accumulated stock.

79/Harbury book: *Bridge of Courage* (Common Courage, 1995).

86–87/rural unions in Brazil: See Biorn Maybury-Lewis, *The Politics of the Possible* (Temple Univ. Press, 1994).

87–88/dispute over PLO: Some excerpts from *Socialist Review* are reprinted in my book *Towards a New Cold War,* p. 430n.

90/Said quote: *The Politics of Dispossession* (Pantheon, 1994).

91/"I wrote about it at the time": *Z* (magazine), 12/90. For a review and a broader context, see the afterword in my *Deterring Democracy* (Hill & Wang, 1992), and *World Orders, Old and New.*

92/Oslo II: For discussion and references, see the epilogue to the 1996 edition of *World Orders, Old and New.*

94/Netanyahu quote: *New York Times,* 7/11/96.

96–97/Shavit op-ed: *New York Times,* 5/27/96. For a full quote of the original passage, see *World Orders, Old and New* (1996 edition), pp. 293–94.

97–98/plundering East Timor's oil: For a discussion and references, see my *Powers and Prospects.*

98–99/Teltsch article: *New York Times,* 12/14/79.

99/*Times* editorial: 12/24/79.

99/Levey article: *Boston Globe,* 1/20/80. I quote and discuss the article in *Towards a New Cold War.*

100/Kohen article: *The Nation,* 11/26/77.

100/media coverage of East Timor: For details, see *Towards a New Cold War,* chap. 13, and my and E. S. Herman's *Political Economy of Human Rights,* vol. 1 (South End, 1979).

100–102/Adam Smith on India: Citations are in my *Year 501: The Conquest Continues* (South End, 1993).

101/Harvard dissertation: Prasannan Parthasarathi (forthcoming as a book).

102–103/Mill on India: *Fraser's Magazine,* November, 1859. Available in Gertrude Himmelfarb, ed., *Essays on Politics and Culture, John Stuart Mill* (Anchor, 1963).

110/Eisenhower quotes: Cited in Robert McMahon, *The Cold War on the Periphery* (Columbia Univ. Press, 1994).

110/Kennan quotes: Cited in my *Year 501,* chap. 5.

111: Merrill book: *Bread and the Ballot: The US and India's Economic Development, 1947-1963* (Univ. of North Carolina Press, 1990).

117/Albright quote: Jules Kagian, *Middle East International* (London), 10/21/94.

118/Mexican tomatoes: *[Added in press]* A year later, the Clinton administration extended long-standing barriers against Japanese supercomputers (Bob Davis, *Wall Street Journal,* 9/29/97). The reasons were similar.

122/new "populism": Richard Berke, "They're Just Regular Ruling Class Guys," *New York Times,* 2/4/96.

124/Tonry book: *Malign Neglect—Race, Crime and Punishment in America* (Oxford Univ. Press, 1995).

128/Raskin book: *New Ways of Knowing: the sciences, society and reconstructive knowledge* (Rowman & Littlefield, 1987).

131/article in *Social Policy*: 9–10/73. Reprinted in *Towards a New Cold War,* chap. 3.

132/*The Fateful Triangle:* (South End, 1983).

132–33/Wolin article: *Dissent,* Summer 1995. My response, Fall 1995.

136/Ferguson book: *Golden Rule,* p. 72 (Univ. of Chicago Press, 1995).

136/Montgomery book: *The Fall of the House of Labor,* p. 7 (Yale Univ. Press, 1987).

138/public opinion about corporations: See my "'Consent without Consent'" *Cleveland State Law Review.*

139/financial transactions: *Globalization in Question.*

144–45/South Commission book: *The Challenge of the South* (1990). I discuss it in *Year 501* and *World Orders, Old and New.*

147/Catholic Church in El Salvador: Leslie Wirpsa, "No-nonsense regime of El Salvador's Sáenz, Cardinal puts brakes on options for the poor in post-Romero church," *National Catholic Reporter,* 4/11/97.

147/Suharto: *[Added in press]* By late 1997, when "our guy" in Jakarta was losing control, he went the way of other failed friends (Marcos, Duvalier, Ceausescu, Mobutu, etc.) and the opposition to him became praiseworthy.

147/"our kind of guy": David Sanger, "Real Politics: Why Suharto Is In and Castro Is Out," *New York Times,* 10/31/95.

150/Vaid book: *Virtual Equality* (Anchor, 1995).

153/Moore book: *Downsize This!* (Crown, 1996).

INDEX

This index covers to the top of page 160; after that, only sections and subsections are indexed. **Boldfaced** *page numbers indicate more substantial discussions, rather than brief mentions.*   *AN*

A

Adler, Sandy, 2

ADM (Archer Daniels Midland), 14

aerospace industry, **30–32**

affirmative action, **10**

affordable housing, groups working to provide, **160**

African-Americans. *See* racism

Ahmad, Eqbal, 87, 89

AIPAC, 96

Albright, Madeleine, 117

"alliance capitalism," 15

Alliance, the, 141

alternative media. *See under* media

Alternative Radio, 4, **191**

Amnesty International, 115

Amos (prophet), **148**

anarchism, 11, 84–85

Andreas, Dwayne, 14

Annan, Kofi, 114

anti-apartheid movement, 143

anticommunism, 41–42

Anti-Defamation League, 96

anti-Semitism, 90, 135

anti-war organizations, **160**

Archer Daniels Midland. *See* ADM

Argentina, **83–86**
  anarchist movement, **84–85**
  independent media, **83–85**
  mass media, 80

Argentina, cont'd.
  more open-minded than US, **85–86**
  neoliberalism in, **84**
  rich out of control, 76
  shantytowns, **83–84**

Aristide, Jean Bertrand, 113

Aristotle, **5–8**

Asia, **87–114**
  groups working on Asian issues, **160–61**
  Also see Central Asian *and* East Asian

"aspirations, domestication of," 146

"attenuation of the shadow," 142

Australia, **98**, 100

B

Baker, James, 33, **91**

Bangladesh, 70, 106

banks launder money, **35–36**

Barger, Brian, 40

Barsamian, David, 2, **4**
  Alternative Radio, 191
  lack of access to East Coast media, 155
  suggests organizations, 159
  visits prison, 37–38

Bates, Greg, 159

Beirut, bombing of, 132

Belo, Carlos, 97

Bengal. *See under* India

Bermuda, 36

Bible, intellectuals in, **148**
Bitter Paradise, 156–57
black market in India, 113–14
blacks, US. *See* racism
BMW, 65
B'nai B'rith, 96
Boeing, 31
Bombay. *See under* India
book publishing, 11–12
Bosch, 65
Boston Globe
　Bernie Sanders op-ed, 29–30
　on East Timor, **99**
　on semiconductors, 15
　on Vietnam War, 47
Boulder (CO), 19, 22–23
Boutros-Ghali, Boutros, 114
Brady, Robert, 63
Brazil, **80–87**
　brutal army, 86
　capital flight, 74–75
　"economic miracle," 56
　favelas, **70–71**, **81–83**
　films in Nova Iguaçu (Rio
　　favela), 52, **81–83**, 153
　foreign debt, **74–75**
　generals, 56, 75
　independent media, 52,
　　80–83, 153
　landless peasants, **86–87**
　left journal, **80**
　mass media, 80
　more open-minded than US,
　　85–86
　rich out of control, 76
　rural workers, **85–87**, 142
　Workers' Party, **86–87**, 141
Bretton Woods system, 67, 73
Bridge of Courage, 79
Brière, Elaine
　cover photo, 2
　film on East Timor, 156
　suggests organizations, 159

British
　East India Company. *See
　　under* India
　in India, 76, **100–103**, **106,
　　109**
　invade Egypt, 68
　protectionist, 101–102, 112
British Columbia, 137
Brown, Ron, 56
Bryant, Adam, 31–32
Buchanan, Pat, 122
budget. *See* federal budget
Buenos Aires, **83–86**
Bush administration,
　position on Israel, **90–91**
　protectionist policies, 15
　weakens OSHA, 37
Bush, George
　anti-Semitic remarks, 90
　"Bou-Bou Ghali," 114
　"new world order," 145
　"what we say, goes," 89
business. *See* corporations
Business Week
　on corporate profits, 25
　"pampered workers," 66
　polls people on business, 61
　on weakening of OSHA, 37

C

Cabral, Amilcar, 145
Calcutta. *See under* India
Cambridge (MA), 156
Campagne, Janee, 159
campaign finance reform.
　See under elections, US
Canada
　Chomsky talks in, 137, 158
　huge demonstration in, 143,
　　NDP, 141
capital flight, **74–77**
capitalism,
　Adam Smith and, 8

capitalism, cont'd.
  de Tocqueville condemns, 9
  future of, **60–62**
  impossibility of, 14
  Jefferson fears, 9
  people's views on, **61–63, 138**
  supposed to be risk-free, 16
  undercuts democracy, 27–28
  wants powerful state, 34
  Also see corporations *and* welfare state
Capitalism and Freedom, 13–14
Carey, Alex, 45
Carnegie, Andrew, 135
Carter, Jimmy, 98
cassette tapes, 156
Castro, Fidel, 79
Center for Constitutional Rights, 9
"center, the vital," 53–54
Central America
  Catholic Church in, 146–47
  democratic institutions, 113
  Jesuits in, **146**
  terror in, 41, **74**, 113
  US solidarity with, 123, 143
Central Asian oil fields, 119
Chevron, **59–60**
Chicago heat wave, 46
Chile, 80, **87**
China, 111
choir, preaching to the, 155
Chomsky, Noam, **4**
  confronts PLO, **87–88**
  criticized in *Dissent,* 132–33
  frequented library as kid, 11
  and *The Nation,* **131–33**
  and *The New York Review of Books,* **129–31**
  suggests organizations, 159

Chomsky, cont'd.
  talks in Vancouver, 137, 158
  on tape, 191
  on WGBH, 50
Chrysler, 30
church groups, **161**
CIA drug running, **39–41**
citations, **172–75**
civil rights groups, **161–62**
civil society
  in Haiti, 54–55
  in US, 23, 37, 55, 144
classical liberalism, 6, 63
Clinton, Bill
  funds jet fighters, 30–31
  as "the last Zionist," 93–94
  in 1996 elections, 53–54
  on Suharto, 147
  wins contract for Exxon, 121–22
Coady, Davida, 159
cocaine, 39–41
college students, 143–44
Colombia, 152
Colorado, 37–38
  Also see Boulder
Columbia University, 151
Columbus, Christopher, 135
common good, the, **5–23**
Communism
  collapse of, 65, 118
  in Eastern Europe, 65–66
  George Soros on, 66–67
  in India, 103–104, 106
  in Indonesia, 110–11, 147
  as necessary enemy, 41–42
community organizing, groups doing, **162**
conservatives, **19–21**
  Also see right, the
Continental Illinois Bank, 30
Contras, 116

cooperate, who's allowed to, 29

Corporate Crime Reporter, 37

corporations, **56–64**
  avoid market discipline, **14–17**
  crime by, **35–37**
  "dazzling" profits, 25
  depend on governments, **14–17**, 73
  executives' job, 57
  executives' liberal views, 23
  former limits on, 20–21
  vs. freedom, 19
  legitimacy of, 20–21, **63–64, 138–39**
  oppose democracy, 53
  people's views on, **61–63, 138**
  power invincible?, **56–64,** 71–73, **138–39**
  profit-making strategies, 57
  propaganda by, 22, **25–28, 43–46,** 55, 62, **121–22, 140–41**
  publications criticizing, **170**
  war against government, 21–22, 26
  welfare for, **29–34**
  Also see wealth *and* welfare states

Council on Foreign Relations, 68

crime, **34–41**
  corporate, **35–37**
  crime rates, 34, 37
  as political issue, 34–35
  S&Ls, 36–37
  Also see drugs

Cuba, 79, 118
  groups working to help, **162**

"culture of terror," 146

current information, list of sources for, **170–71**

Czech Republic, 65–66, 118–19

D

Daimler-Benz, 21, 65

Daniels, Ron, 9

Dark Alliance, 40

Davos (Switzerland), 67

Dayan, Moshe, 96

Deadly Deception, 50

debt
  East Asian vs. Latin American, 76
  myth of Third World, **74–77,** 154

"defense." *See* Pentagon *and* weapons manufacturers

democracy
  and extremes of wealth, **6–8**
  and the market, 8
  and the media, **50–51**
  must be welfare state, 6
  opposition to, **7–8,** 23, 25, 45, 48, 53, 54, 67, **113**
  participatory, **6–8**
  preventing functioning of, 7
  the threat of, **7–8,** 53

Democratic Party, 26, **53–54**

de Tocqueville, Alexis
  on equality in US, 9
  fear of "manufacturing aristocracy," 9
  hypocrisy of, 102
  on wealth vs. democracy, 6

Dewey, John, **141–42**

Dhaka (Bangladesh), 106

Disney, 137

"disposable people," 124

Dissent, 132–33

dissent, manufacturing, **153–58**

Dole, Bob, 53–54

domestic affairs, **24–64**

"domestication of aspirations," 146

do Rego, Leoneto, 98–99
Downsize This!, 153
drugs
  can't stop flow of, 55
  CIA involvement, **39–41**
  money laundering, **35–36**
  traffickers as the enemy, 42
  war on, **35, 39, 124**

E

East Asian foreign debt, 76
Eastern Europe
  back to Third World status,
    65–66, 118–19
  as source of cheap labor, 66
East India Company. *See
  under* India
East Timor, **97–100**
  film on, 156
East Timor Action Network,
  100
economic
  conversion, organizations
    working for, **160**
  justice, organizations
    working for, **163**
  "miracles," 56
  publications, **170**
editor's note, 4
Egypt, 68, 77
Eisenhower, Dwight, 110
elections, US, **53–56**
  as auctions, 55
  campaign finance reform,
    55–56
  1996, **53–54**
  1924, 54
El Salvador, 146–47
endnotes, **172–75**
enemies, necessary, **41–42**
Energy, Department of, 32
Enlightenment, the, 6, 63

environmental
  information, **163**
  publications, **171**
  regulations avoided, 16
equality, **8–10**
Ericsson, 33
evangelical religion, 53
"expanding the floor of the
    cage," **85**, 142
explanatory notes, 4
Exxon, 121–22

F

Fanon, Franz, 145
Farrakhan, Louis, 123–24
far right, 23
Fateful Triangle, The, 132
favelas. See under Brazil
federal budget, **29–30**
Ferguson, Thomas, 136
Fidelity Investments, **20–21**
financial speculation, 57, 73
Financial Times, 65–66
Finkelstein, Norman, 93
Firestone Tire and Rubber,
    59–60
Fisk, Robert, 115
FitzGerald, Frances, 131
"flexibility," 56
Flint (MI), **27–28**
Forbes, Steve, 122
Ford, Henry, 56
foreign affairs, **65–119**
foreign debt. *See* debt
Fortune
  on corporate profits, 25
  500, 57
  100, 14
foundationalism, 127–28
1492, 500th anniversary, 135

France
  demonstrations in, 142
  invades Egypt, 68
  labor in, 140
freedom, **13–23**
  corporations threaten, 19
"free trade," **16–17**
Friedman, Milton, 13–14
Friedman, Thomas, **71–72**
Fugh-Berman, Adrienne, 159
funding organizations, **163–64**

G

Gates, Bill, 67
GATT, 117
"Gay Nineties," 135
gay rights, 137
Gaza. See under Israel
General Electric, 50, 67
General Motors
  in conspiracy, **59–60**
  in Flint (MI), 27
  foreign investments, 21, 66
Germany
  corporations based there,
    21, 65
  demonstrations in, 142
  financial significance, 139
  labor, 21, 65–66
  unemployment, 65
Ghandi, Indira, 104
Gingrich, Newt
  attends conference, 67
  hypocrisy of, 72
  and Lockheed, 30
Gitlin, Todd, 122–23
globalization, **65–73**
  early in 20th century, 73
  resistance to, 69–70, **72–73**
government
  corporate war on, 21–22
  the need to make use of it
    (at this point), **84–85**

government, cont'd.
  subsidizes business, **29–34**
  under public control (to
    some extent), 139
  works for the rich, 138
Green Party, 141
Greider, William, 77
Grossman, Richard, 63
Guaraní, 83
Guatemala, **79–80**
Gulf War, 89
Gusmao, Xanana, 97

H

Haiti
  civil society in, 54–55
  democratic institutions, 113
  poverty in, 60, 70
  US hostility to, 113
Hamilton, Alexander, 8
Harbury, Jennifer, 79
hard times, myth of, **24–29**
Harlem, 70
Harvard, 101, 135
health
  in Eastern Europe, 66
  groups working on, **165–66**
  in Kerala, 104
  struggle for health care, 136
  US vs. Third World, 71
Hebron. See under Israel
Helms-Burton Act, 118
Herbert, Robert, 43
Heritage Foundation, 18
Herman, Edward S., **42–43**
high-tech. See science and
  technology
Hitchens, Christopher,
  124–25
Holocaust Museum, 96–97
Homestead (PA), 135, 136
Hoover Institute, 19–20

Horton, Willie, 124

Howe, Florence, 129

human rights organizations, **166**

Hungary, 118–19

I

"illuminati, the" (NYC left intellectuals), **129–33**

IMF (International Monetary Fund), 78

import restrictions. *See* protectionism

India, **100–114**
  Adam Smith on, **100–102**
  advertising agencies in, 69, 107–108
  Bengal, **100–101**, **106, 109**
  black market, 113–14
  Bombay slums, 70, 103
  British in, 76, **100–103**, **106, 109**
  Calcutta, 104
  Communist governments, 103–104, 106
  East India Company, 100–102
  famine, 111
  feudal attitudes, 112–13
  Hyderabad, 112
  industry crushed, **100–101**
  inefficiency in, 113–14
  intellectual property rights, **108**
  Kashmir, 106
  Kerala, **103–104, 106**
  media ownership, 107
  Mutiny of 1857, 103
  neoliberalism in, **106–110**, 112
  neutralism of, **110–11**
  peasant struggle, 104
  poverty, 70, 103
  recruitment of scientists, **108–109**
  reservations system, 10

India, cont'd.
  resists foreign domination, 69
  US attitudes toward, **110–11**
  village self-government, **103–105**
  wars with Pakistan, 110
  West Bengal, **103–105**, 113, 152

Indians (American). *See* native population

Indonesia
  Communism in, 110–11, 147
  and East Timor, **97–100**
  gives Exxon contract, 121–22
  massacre in, 110–11, 147
  might infect Asia, **110–11**
  NY Times criticizes, 43

information, list of sources for current, **170–71**

Inquiry, 100

intellectual property rights, 17, **108**

intellectuals
  in the Bible, **148**
  New York leftist, **129–33**
  responsibility of, 153–54

International Labor Organization, 62, **116**

International Monetary Fund. *See* IMF

international organizations, **114–19**

Internet, 49–50, **149**

investment industry, 20–21

Iraq, 117

Israel, **87–97**
  Allon plan, 92
  and American Jews, **94–97**
  Baker plan, 91
  Bantustans in, 93
  Beirut, bombing of, 132
  Gaza, 92, 95

Israel, cont'd.
  Gush Katif, 92
  Hebron, 93
  invades Egypt, 68
  invades Lebanon, **96**
  Jerusalem, 90, **94**
  Occupied Territories, 88,
    90–95
  Oslo II agreement, 92
  Palestinian Authority, **92–93**
  Palestinians massacred, 132
  Palestinian "state," 93
  Sabra and Shatila
    (Lebanon), 132
  West Bank settlements,
    90–95
  Also see Mideast *and* PLO

J

Jailer, Todd, 159
Japan
  foreign debt, 76
  import restrictions, 112
  invests in Vietnam, 79
  and semiconductors, **15–17**
jargon, 128, 153
Jay, John, quote by, 7
Jefferson, Thomas
  and capitalism, 8
  fear of "manufacturing
    aristocracy," 9
  on wealth vs. democracy, 6
Jerusalem. *See under* Israel
Jesuits, Central American, **146**
Jewish National Fund, 95
Jews, American, and Israel,
  94–97
"jobs," not "profits," **121–22**
Jones, Mother, 136
Jordan, 91

K

Kashmir. *See under* India
Katz, Sheila, 159
Kennan, George, 110

Kennedy, John F., 143
Kentucky Fried Chicken, 69
Kerala. *See under* India
Keynes, John Maynard, 127
Kissinger, Henry, **129–31**, 158
Knesset, 94
Kohen, Arnold, **100**
Korea. *See* South Korea
Korol, Richard, 2
Korsch, Karl, 120

L

labor
  in Canada, 143
  "clear subjugation of," 27
  coopted by business, **27–28**
  demonstrations, 143
  in France, 140, 143
  in Germany, 21, 65–66, 143
  hurt by "workfare," 26
  international standards, 62
  Labor Party, 141
  newspapers (former), 50–51
  organizations, **166**
  publications, **171**
  reporters, 51
  rights guaranteed by, 19
  strikes in South Korea, 62
  struggles for rights, **135–36**
  are unions necessary?, 56
  workers used to use
    libraries, 11, 13
  Also see International Labor
    Organization

Latin America, **77–87**
  Catholic Church in, 146–47
  "disposable people" in, 124
  foreign debt and, 76
  Jesuits in, 146
  organizations working to
    help, **166–67**
  publications on, **171**
  Also see Central America
    and individual countries

Lauter, Paul, 129
Lebanon, Israel invades, **96**
left, the US, **120–58**
  meaningful term?, **120–22**
Lenin, V. I., 149–50
Leninism, 120
Lewis, Anthony, **46–48**
Levey, Robert, 99
Lexington (MA), 12–13
liberals
  alive and well, 5
  vs. conservatives, **19–21**
  decline of, **26–29**
  in the media, **42–46**
  Also see classical liberalism
    and left, the
libraries, **11–13**
Libya, 42
Lincoln, Edward, 15
Lockheed, 30, 31
Los Angeles, **59–60**
Lula, **86–87**
Luxemburg, Rosa, 120
Lyons, Louis M., 50

M

Madison, James, **7–8**
magic answer, the, **149–53**
Manufacturing Consent
  dedicated to Alex Carey, 45
  film, 50
  five news filters, 41, **173n41**
  function of the media, **42**
manufacturing dissent,
  153–58
"market discipline," 108
Marseilles, 40
Marxism
  left, 11, 120
  traditional, 60
Marx, Karl, 149

Massachusetts
  progressive thinking in,
    61–62, 151–52
  "tax relief" for corporations,
    20
Mathematics for the Millions,
  128
Mattick, Paul, 120
Maxwell, Jane, 159
McCallister, Susan, 2, 159
McChesney, Robert, **48–51**
McCoy, Alfred W., 40
McDonnell Douglas, 31
McGovern, Jim, 5
media, the, **41–53**
  access to, 50, **155–56**
  alternative, 52, **80–83**, 153,
    156–57, **167**, 191
  in Argentina, 80, 83
  better (but still bad), 50
  in Brazil, 52, **80–83**, 153
  in Chile, 80
  commercial-free, 52
  community access TV, 156
  coverage of labor, **50–51**
  democratic, **50–51**, 52
  and East Timor, **97–100**
  five news filters, **173n41**
  function of, **42**
  groups working to change,
    167–68
  in India, 107
  as liberal, **42–46**
  as propaganda system,
    43–46, **121–22**, 156–57
  publications on, **170–71**
  public broadcasting, **48–51**
  television, effect on society,
    52–53
Merrill, Dennis 111
Merrill Lynch, 32
Mexico
  bailout, 16
  financial collapse, **77–78**

Mexico, cont'd.
tomato exports, 118
"trade" with, 16
Also see Zapatistas
Mideast, **87–97**
groups working on, **168**
and *The Nation,* 131–32
oil reserves, 89–90
"peace process," **44**, **90–95**
publication on, **171**
Also see Israel *and* PLO
military. *See* Pentagon *and*
weapons manufacturers
Mill, James, 102
Mill, John Stuart, **102–103**
Million Man March, **123–24**
MIT, 4, 104
Mokhiber, Russell, 37
money laundering, **35–36**
Moore, Michael, 153
Morehouse, Ward, 63
Mudge, Naomi, 159
Multinational Monitor, 34
myths
hard times are here, **24–29**
media are objective, **41–53**
Third World debt, **74–77**
Thomas Friedman's, 71–72
US favors democracy, 7–158

N

Nader, Ralph, 26, 141
NAFTA, 51, 118
Naiman, Arthur, 2
notes by, 4, 159–60, 170,
172, 176
suggests organizations, 159
"narcissism of small
differences," 122–23
Nassar, Gamal Abd al-, 145
Nation, The, **131–32**, 142–43
native population (of Western Hemisphere), **134**

NATO (North Atlantic Treaty
Organization), **118–19**
Navasky, Victor, **131–32**
NDP, 141
Nehru, Jawaharlal, **110–11**,
145
neoliberalism
in Argentina, **84**
in India, **106–110**, 112
in Mexico, **77–78**
Netanyahu, Benjamin, 67, 94
New Deal, 5, 8
New Party, 141
Newton, Isaac, **126–27**
"new world order," 145
New York City
left intellectuals in, **129–33**
schools, 37
"workfare" in, 26
New York Review of Books,
129–31
New York Times
Ari Shavit op-ed, **96–97**
and East Timor, **98–99**
improvements at, 43
on Indonesia, 43
on "industrial military
complex," 31–32
lack of improvement at, 48
on NAFTA, **51–52**
on new "populism," 122
op-ed on liberals vs.
conservatives, **19–21**
on postmodernism, 126
Thomas Friedman in, **71–72**
on Vatican's impact in
Latin America, 146
on Vietnam War, **46–48**
New York University, 125
NGO (defined), 81
Nicaragua, 116, 171
1984, 38

Nixon, Richard
  destroys Vietnam, **129–31**
  last liberal president, 26
Nkrumah, Kwame, 145
Nobel Peace Prize, 4, 97
nonaligned movement,
  144–47
Noriega, Manuel, 41
notes, **172–75**
Nova Iguaçu, **81–83**
NPR (National Public Radio),
  14, 156
Nye, Joseph, 68

O

Occupied Territories. *See
  under* Israel
Odonian Press, 2, 192
OECD, 36
oil (petroleum)
  off East Timor, 98
  in India, 111
  in the Mideast, 89–90
One World, Ready or Not, 77
opportunity, equality of, **8–10**
Opus Dei, 147
organizations worth
  supporting, list of, **159–69**
Ortiz, Dianna, 79
Orwell, George, 38, 133
OSHA, 37
Oslo II. *See under* Israel
outsourcing, 24
Owens, William, 68

P

Pakistan, 110
Palestinians. *See under* Israel.
  Also see PLO.
Panama, 36
Panama Deception, The, 50
Pannekoek, Anton, 120

Paraguay, 83
Parks, Rosa, 139–40
Parry, Robert, 40
participatory democracy, **6–8**
patents, 17, **108**
PBS (Public Broadcasting
  System), 14
Penn Central, 30
Pentagon
  as conduit for high-tech
    investment, **30–33**
  people's views on, 22
  right-wing support of, 12, 18
  as subsidy for rich, 12
Pentagon Papers, **46–48**
Perot, Ross, 72
Perry, William, 31
"personal is political," 124–25
petroleum. *See* oil
Philadelphia (PA), 4, 11
PKI, 147
PLO (Palestinian Liberation
  Organization), **87–88**
  Also see Israel *and* Mideast
Poland, 65–66, 118–19
political change, strategies
  for, 60, **134–58**
political parties and groups,
  141–42, 168
poor, the. *See* poverty
populism, phony, 122
Port of Spain (Trinidad), 58–59
Portugal, 98, 99
postmodernism, **125–28**
poverty
  and democracy, **6–8**
  in Haiti, 60, 70
  in India vs. US, 70–71
  War on Poverty, 28
  welfare, **25–26**, 124
preaching to the choir, 155

"preferential option for the poor," 146
prisons, funding for, **37–38**
"profits" now called "jobs," **121–22**
progress, signs of, (and not), **134–39, 143–47**
Progressive Caucus, 5
Prohibition, 39
propaganda
  corporate, 22, **25–28**, 55, 62, **140–41**
  media as propaganda system, **43–46**, **121–22**, 156–57
  against Social Security, 29
  for Telecommunications Act of 1996, 49
  Also see media
prophets, false and true, **148**
protectionism
  British, 101–102, 112
  good or bad, 112
  in 19th c. US, 101–102, 112
  patents used for, 108
  by Reagan administration, 15, 33
public
  broadcasting. *See under* media
  control of government, 139
  funding for science and technology, 23, 33
  services in '30s and '40s, 11
  transportation, 13, **59–60**
publishing, 11–12
Putnam, Robert, 52–53, 144

Q

Qana (Lebanon), 115
Quakers, **157–58**

R

racism
  in Brazil, 82

racism, cont'd.
  in the US, 10, 114, **123–24**, 135–36
radical alternatives, 62
  Also see left, the
radio. *See* media
Ramos-Horta, José, 97
Ramparts, 131
Raskin, Marc, 128
Raytheon, **20–21**
Reagan administration
  military funding, 33
  protectionism, 15, 33
  weakens OSHA, 37
Reagan, Ronald
  clueless, 33
  vs. "Libyan hit squads," 42
  on welfare, 124
"really existing market theory," 17
Real Story series, 192
Reich, Robert, 56
religion, evangelical, 53
Republican Party, 26
research organizations, **168**
resistance to oppression, **139–48**
rich, the. *See* wealth
right, the US
  far right, 23
  vs. liberals, **19–21**
  meaningful term?, **120–22**
  opposes free libraries, 12
  supports the Pentagon, 12
Rio de Janeiro, 81, 156
"Roaring Twenties," 136
Rockefeller, David, 79
Roosevelt, Franklin D., 8
Rosene, Chris, 159
Rothbard, Murray, 18
Russell, Bertrand, 120

Russia, 119
Ryan, Randolph, 46–47

S

Sabra and Shatila (Lebanon), 132
Said, Edward
  confronts PLO, 87
  on hypocrisy, 102
  opposes US-Israeli policy, 96
  quoted on Mideast, 90
Sanders, Bernie, 29–30
S&Ls, 36–37
San Jose Mercury News, **39–41**
São Paulo, 80
Scheiner, Charlie, 100
schools, underfunded, **37–38**
Schurmann, Franz, 129
science and technology
  and prisons, 38
  public funding for, 23, 33
Scott, Peter Dale, 129
Sematech consortium, 15
semiconductors, **15–17**
Shavit, Ari, **96–97**
shantytowns, **70–71, 81–84**
Shaw, Maya, 159
Siemens, 65
signs of progress (and not), **134–39, 143–47**
Silvers, Robert, **130–31**
Singer, Daniel, 142–43
slums, 11, **70–71,**
  Also see shantytowns
Smith, Adam
  and capitalism, 8
  on equality, 9
  on India, **100–102**
  on wealth vs. democracy, 6
Smith, Gar, 159

smoking
  and freedom, 17, **19**
  now lower-class, 39
socially responsible investing, 63
Social Policy, 131
Social Security "reform," **28–29**
Social Text, 125
Socrates, 148
Sokal, Allen, 125
Somalia, 114–15
Soros, George, 66–67
sources for current information, **170–71**
sources for facts in book, **172–75**
South Commission, **144–45**
South Korea, 62, 76, 112
Soviet Union, 65, 118
  Also see Russia
Spain, newspapers in, 6
speaking truth to power, **157–58**
speculation. *See* financial speculation
Stalinism, 19
Standard Oil of California. *See* Chevron
state level, shifting power to, 21–22
Strange Disappearance of Civic America, The, **52–53**
structural adjustment. *See* neoliberalism
students, 143–44
Suharto, Thojib, 147
Sukarno, Ahmed, 145
Sweden, 33–34
Sweeney, John, 68

T

Taiwan, 76, 112

Taking the Risk out of Democracy, 45

tape
cassettes as alternative media, 156
Chomsky on, 191

tariffs. *See* protectionism

taxes, avoided, 16, 20–21

technology. *See* science and technology

telecommunications
Act of 1996, 49
government subsidizes, 68
revolution in, 67, 73

television. *See under* media

Teltsch, Kathleen, 98–99

"terror, culture of," 146

Tet offensive, 47

Third World
debt not really owed, **74–77**
groups that help, **168–69**
health in, 66, 71, 104
more open-minded than US, **75–76,** 85–86, 154
solidarity with, 121, 123
US coming to resemble, 35
will whole world become like?, 61
working conditions, **57–59**
Also see Eastern Europe, Latin America, Mideast *and individual countries*

Timor. *See* East Timor

Tito, Josip Broz, 145

tobacco. *See* smoking

Tonry, Michael, 124

"trade," misuse of term, 16

transnationals. *See* corporations

Trilateral Commission, **67–68**

Trinidad, 58–59

Trotsky, Leon, 120, 149–50

Truman, Harry S, 111

truth to power, speaking, **157–58**

TV Nation, 153

Tweedledum and Tweedledee, 26

Twilight of Common Dreams, The, 122

U

UCLA, 143

UN (and abbreviations beginning with UN-). *See under* United Nations

unions. See *labor*

United Nations, **114–17**
Development Program, 14, 116
Food and Agriculture Program, 116
as tool of US, **114–15**
UNCTAD, 116
UNESCO, 116
US hostility toward, **114–15**

United States
becoming like Third World, 35
close-minded, **75–76,** 85–86, 154
domestic affairs, **10 64**
dominates world culture, 69–70
and East Timor, **97–100**
foreign investments, **35–36**
ignores international law, 62
impact abroad, **65–119**
and Israel, **89–91, 93–97**
left in, **120–33**
opposition to democracy, **113**
origins of political system, 7–8

United States, cont'd.
  scapegoats UN, **114–15**
  in 21st century, 68
Upper West Side (NYC), 129
Uruguay Round, 117
USSR. *See* Soviet Union

V

Vaid, Urvashi, 150
Vancouver (BC), 137, 158
Vanity Fair, 124
Vatican, the, 146–47
Vermont, 29
Vietnam
  bombing of, 130, 143
  Boston Globe on war, **47**
  Chomsky visits, 50
  Japanese investment in, 79
  Nixon and Kissinger lie to,
    129–31
  NY Times on war, **46-48**
  US punishes after war, 79
village self-government in
  India, **103–105**
Virtual Equality, 150

W

Wall Street Journal, 20, 126
war on drugs. *See under* drugs
War on Poverty, 28
Washington Post, 22
wealth, **6–8,** 25
  Also see corporations
weapons manufacturers,
  20–21, **30–33**
Webb, Gary, **39–41**
Welch, John, 67
welfare, **25–26,** 124
welfare states
  democracies must be, 6
  in Flint (MI), 27
  in Sweden, 33–34

Wellstone, Paul, 5
West Bank. *See under* Israel
West Bengal. *See under* India
WGBH (Boston), 50
what you can do, **134–69**
Winship, Tom, 47
Witness for Peace, 121
Wolin, Richard, 132–33
women
  in Argentina, 83–84
  groups working on
    women's issues, **169,** 171
  in India, 104–105, 113
  win rights, 54, 135
workers. *See* labor
Workers' Party. *See under*
  Brazil
"workfare" in New York, 26
World Bank (in Mexico), 78
World Court, **116**
World Economic Forum, 67
World Orders, Old and New
  critiqued in *Dissent,* 132–33
  on Palestinians, 93, 94
  on the UN, 114
"world trade," 16
World Trade Organization,
  17, **117–18**

Y

Yad Vashem, 96–97
Yugoslavia (former), 115

Z

Z (magazine), 42, 44
Zapatistas, 72, **78–79**
Z Papers, 128
Zinn, Howard
  doesn't whine, 153
  says change takes time, 151
  visits prison, 37
Zionism. *See* Israel